LUCK

Playing Hardball
On and Off the Field
What Sport Tells Us About Life

LUCK

What it Means and Why it Matters

ED SMITH

BLOOMSBURY
LONDON · NEW DELHI · NEW YORK · SYDNEY

First published in Great Britain 2012

Copyright © 2012 by Edward Smith

The moral right of the author has been asserted

No part of this book may be used or reproduced in any manner whatsoever
without written permission from the Publisher except in the case of brief
quotations embodied in critical articles or reviews

Bloomsbury Publishing Plc
50 Bedford Square
London
WC1B 3DP

www.bloomsbury.com

Bloomsbury Publishing, London, New Delhi, New York and Sydney

A CIP catalogue record for this book is available from the British Library

ISBN 978 1 4088 1547 2 (hardback edition)
ISBN 978 1 4088 2657 7 (trade paperback edition)

10 9 8 7 6 5 4

Typeset by Hewer Text UK Ltd, Edinburgh

Printed in Great Britain by Clays Ltd, St Ives plc

MIX
Paper from
responsible sources
FSC® C018072

For Rebecca

CONTENTS

Part 1

Experience

I

Improbability

I

I am the least likely person to be writing a book about luck. For most of my life, I haven't believed in it at all. I thought that talking about luck was an admission of weakness. I confidently – or naively – believed that you made your own luck. If you were good enough for long enough, you got what you deserved. I bridled at the suggestion that 'We all need some luck.' Luck was for other people.

Most kids cheer for the talented showman – Ian Botham, Paul Gascoigne or Daley Thompson. Not me. My childhood hero was an obdurate, balding man who wore glasses when he played sport: the tough, flinty Yorkshireman Geoff Boycott.

Why Boycott? Sure, Boycott was brilliant. And I may have picked up a touch of my Yorkshire grandfather's county pride. But it was something else that led me to Boycott. Even as a child, I sensed there was something in Boycott that was different – an application of willpower, an elimination of error, an unbendingness and relentlessness. I think all those traits appealed deeply to my over-developed sense of rationality and ambition. Could a child possibly sense in a hero something of himself? It sounds silly, doesn't it? But I think it is true.

It is almost inevitable that future professional cricketers were first mad-keen youngsters. But very few, I expect, stood in front of the television as a four-year-old, front forearm wrapped in a white paper bag to replicate the Boycott armguard, trying to emulate the great master's forward defence: implacable, controlled, defiant, solitary. Not a very jolly form of hero-worship, is it?

But this is exactly how I spent long stretches of childhood. I created an alternative world and inhabited it. Central to my life as a child was creating an imaginary world, a cricketing fantasy in which I always succeeded. Alone in the TV room, Test match on, bat in hand, opponents clear in my mind, technique honed, strategy decided upon. Hours, days, summers all passed with me absorbed in that world. It used to amuse me – much later, in the grown-up world – when sports psychologists told me to practise 'positive visualization'. I'd been at it since I was four.

Batting easily lends itself to metaphor: the innings of a lifetime. How should we bat, how should we live? Boycott stood firmly at one end of the spectrum, taking self-absorption to the limits of sanity. Eyes always on the ball, but only on the ball, never straying to consider the view of the boundary, still less the world beyond it. The Boycott mantra was to retain control, eliminate risk and dictate your own destiny. Even now, Boycott is fond of reminiscing about his contempt for the idea of luck. 'Dennis Amiss used to say, "Good luck" to me. I used to reply, "It's not luck but ability that counts."'

No wonder the phrase 'Leave nothing to chance' is a favourite of modern sports psychologists. They make a virtue not only of the Boycott mindset but also of the Boycott worldview. Ours is the age of ultra-specialization, of eliminating unnecessary distractions, of focusing in and narrowing down. As Boycott himself put it, 'I loved batting and I do not use the word lightly ... everything else had to come second.'

I was like that, too: obsessive, relentless and analytical. My bedroom walls were decorated with a series of posters from the MCC coaching manual. The last thing I saw at night as I closed my eyes to go to sleep was a poster entitled, 'How to play the perfect forward defence'. That nerdy streak coexisted with the sociability of the natural show-off. My dad was a brilliant teacher in many respects, but even he couldn't teach me much modesty. It makes me laugh, thinking about it now, to reflect on the contrast between the two of us: the modest father, who would rather do anything than boast, and the immodest son, never happier than when he was recounting recent triumphs.

So when I started playing competitive matches as an eight-year-old, Dad didn't only coach me how to bat, he also coached me about modesty. He had more success in the first than the second.

One day, when we were watching a Kent match together, Dad saw his friend Sir (as he was then) Colin Cowdrey walking towards us. Dad grasped the probability that his cricket-mad son would launch into a long monologue about his own talent as soon as the great man arrived. 'Now listen, Ed,' Dad began. 'We're about to bump into Colin Cowdrey, one of the greatest players England has ever produced. As he is very polite, he will probably ask about your cricket. Try to be modest. So if he says, "Are you a batter or a bowler?" you might say, "Oh, a little bit of both" or something like that. Downplay things. Remember: modesty.'

I nodded as if to say, 'Message received. No problem.'

Colin duly arrived and, with his customary charm, immediately enquired about my cricket. Exactly as Dad had predicted, Colin wondered if I was more of a batter or a bowler. 'It's hard to say,' I replied. Dad looked hopeful. I think he began to mouth the words 'A-little-bit-of-both', trying to prod me in the right direction.

I had better ideas. 'It's hard to say, Colin,' I continued, lightly assuming first-name terms. 'Because I am a genuine all-rounder. You see, I open both the batting and the bowling. For example, last Saturday ...'

My father's hopeful expression evaporated, and his eyes were magnetically drawn to his own shoes, where they remained fixed until he could think of a convenient excuse to whisk me into the club shop to buy a scorecard and relieve

Colin of listening to every shot I'd played on the way to 64 not out for my under-nines' team.

I was always clear where I was going. There was a straight line ahead and nothing would get in the way. Teams became staging posts in a grand sweep of ambition. First my school, then Kent schools, then Cambridge University, then the Kent professional team, finally the full England side. Each time I assumed I'd get a hundred on debut. Anything less would be failure. Then I'd move on to the next team, the level higher, a new challenge – upwards indefinitely, never pausing to doubt myself or stopping to settle for what I already had.

Talent plus effort equals merit. That was the sociologist Michael Young's definition of *meritocracy*, a word he invented. (Later we'll see how far the modern definition has moved from Young's satirical intention.) If I had known about the word as a child, I would have passionately believed in it. My view was simple: if you had ability and you practised enough, nothing could stop you.

When I abandoned playing the cello at the age of fourteen, the reason I gave was a cold calculation of meritocratic potential. I told my music teacher I wanted more time to focus on cricket. 'I can't be the best at playing the cello,' I explained, sounding like a Geoff Boycott in waiting. 'But I can be the best at playing cricket.' It sounded so tough and self-deterministic at the time, as though nothing else should enter into how you choose hobbies and pastimes. Luck – in either success or failure – didn't come into it at all.

I took my contempt for the idea of luck into early adult life. At Cambridge, I took the same approach to studying history as I did to my cricket. I don't think I felt pressure on myself. Success was just an imperative. I refused even to contemplate failure. The right combination of ability and hard work, I believed, surely made success inevitable. I wanted the perfect game, the perfect life: a game free from contingency, a life with nothing left to chance.

What did luck have to do with anything? I would have wholeheartedly agreed with my childhood hero Geoff Boycott. Luck was for other people.

II

Bizarrely, my dismissal of luck coexisted with obsessive superstition. By my mid-teens, I was profoundly superstitious. It wasn't just not walking under ladders. I couldn't walk past a slightly dripping tap without stopping to force it completely closed, couldn't change seats in the class-room on match-days, couldn't wear a different shirt from the one I'd worn the previous week (if I'd played well, that is).

Because I got a hundred on my school debut, everything I did that day became fixed in stone. So I couldn't walk out to bat with my opening partner on the 'wrong' side of me, couldn't put my right leg-guard on before my left, couldn't swap corners in the changing room, wouldn't take off my cricket sweater even if I was too hot. Not mid-innings, anyway. Never change a winning formula.

Saturdays – the whole day, not just the hours of play – were especially defined by superstition. In my mind, everything that happened was part of a chain of causes that determined how many runs I would get in the match. Messing up one part of the chain interfered with the end result.

This conviction coexisted alongside a childish faith in just deserts, the idea that I had to deserve success, not just through practice but also through behaviour. The combination of superstition and just deserts had some strange consequences. When I picked up my cricket kit on Saturdays, I couldn't walk past something that needed tidying up without stopping and doing it right away. Even flippant remarks might end up getting me into trouble with the cricketing gods. So Saturdays were good for my mother as well as (usually) for me. I should not make myself out to sound better than I was. Conveniently, I behaved as though the cricketing gods observed my domestic manners less closely on Sundays, Mondays, Tuesdays, Wednesdays, Thursdays and Fridays.

I was still superstitious when I got to university. Before my first game for Cambridge in 1996, I stopped off at the news-agent across the street, buying a paper and a can of Lucozade Sport. I cycled to the ground, kit on my back, sat in my corner seat in the dressing room, drinking my fizzy drink and reading *The Times*, with my cricket bats (there were only two in those days) lined up neatly in front of me.

I got a hundred on first-class debut for Cambridge, too. At eighteen years and nine months, I was the youngest person ever to do that. The result? Apart from getting me off to a good start in my career, that hundred sold plenty of cans of Lucozade and copies of *The Times* for that paper shop. After all, how could I possibly change my routine now? It didn't change much from my first match for Cambridge to my last.

The problem with superstitions is that they become both addictive and cumulative. It is far easier to add new superstitions than to lose old ones. By my early twenties, playing regularly for Kent, I accumulated a ridiculously long routine of pre-ball rituals that I performed before *every ball I received*. I'd wipe my forehead with the thumb of my glove, I'd touch the peak of my batting helmet, I'd push down the Velcro on each glove, I'd rearrange my thigh-pad. Remember, you receive on average eighty balls in a typical innings. So on a good day, when I might bat for three times as long as the average, I could knock off two hundred sets of rituals as well as a hundred runs.

Every time, the order would be the same, the rhythm would be the same, the ritual identical. My dependence on superstitious rituals came dangerously close to slowing down the tempo of the whole match. As with Jonathan Trott, the current England batter, bowlers would often have to wait while I finished my routine.

As if that wasn't enough, after the fourth ball of every six-ball over, I would ask the umpire how many balls were left in the over. I nearly always knew what the answer would be – two. But I asked anyway and (nearly always) the umpire was happy to fall into step with my routine. Somewhere in the middle of my career, I switched to asking the umpire after the third ball of the over. So the answer was three. Always 'Three left, Ed.' I reckon I batted for about 15,000 overs in my career. So I must have asked the umpire whether there were two, or three, balls left in the over 15,000 times.

How can I explain it? It was silly and I knew it. It was unintelligent and I knew it. It was a source of mirth and I knew it. But I did it anyway. Superstition was a dependency I found hard to give up.

A case can be made in favour of superstition, of course. Success in sport depends on successfully repeating a series of actions and movements. Sportsmen not only groove physical technique until it is second nature. Mental skills require endless practice, too, and routine is often a powerful tool that helps concentration.

My father is a novelist and playwright who still writes in long-hand – with soft pencils and paper rather than mouse, keyboard and computer. When he periodically sharpens a dozen pencils, one after the other, his physical actions inter-act with his mental state. He is sending signals to his mind: I am switching on as a writer, I am readying myself. I suppose I was doing something with all that scratching and fiddling around before each ball. My superstitious routine had become bound up with the way I concentrated. It was both rational and irrational simultaneously.

But superstition can clearly trip over into near madness. The former table-tennis player Matthew Syed explores the psychology of superstition in an excellent chapter in his book *Bounce*. Goran Ivanišević became convinced that if he won a match, he had to duplicate his actions precisely prior to the next one. He had to eat in the same restaurant, even watch the same television programmes. During one Wimbledon tournament, he had to watch the children's show *Teletubbies* every morning.

You'd expect that most sportsmen would be able to find time to meet the Queen. But the unfailingly courteous Rafael Nadal had to skip his royal appointment during the 2010 Wimbledon because he *hadn't* met the Queen the day before. He couldn't face interfering with a winning pattern of behaviour. Given the choice between the Queen and his winning routine, routine won in straight sets.

The South African cricketer Neil McKenzie became convinced that he would perform well only if he attached his spare cricket bats to the ceiling of the changing room using adhesive tape. The baseball player Jim Ohms put a coin in his jockstrap after every winning match. By the end of the season, opponents would hear the clang of the coins as he ran towards base. The brilliant Australian rugby winger David Campese insisted he sat next to the bus driver during the journey to every away match. The striking thing is that superstition hobbles even the coolest players. Swerving, swaggering 'Campo' Campese always looked like the most relaxed man on the pitch. Now we learn he was fretting about where he sat on the team bus.

You could argue that superstition may provide sportsmen extra self-belief. But superstition can just as easily become a burden. When Venus Williams suffered a surprise defeat in the 2008 French Open, she had a novel explanation: 'I didn't tie my laces right and I didn't bounce the ball five times and I didn't bring my shower sandals to the court with me. I didn't have my extra dress. I knew it was just fate; it wasn't going to happen.' When Kolo Touré was playing for Arsenal, he insisted on being the last player to leave the dressing room after half-time. So when his team-mate William Gallas needed medical treatment, Touré refused to leave the room before him. Arsenal had to start the second half with nine players rather than eleven.

What is going on here? The psychologist B. F. Skinner placed some hungry pigeons in a cage and fed them at random intervals. The pigeons linked the first arrival of food with the actions they were performing at the time. To the pigeons, this 'link' remained fixed, even though it failed to influence the arrival of food in the future. So Skinner noted that one bird 'repeatedly thrust its head into one of the upper corners of the cage', while another 'developed a "tossing" response, as if placing its head beneath an invisible bar and lifting it repeatedly'. As Syed concludes: 'Both the pigeons and the players witnessed a random connection between a particular type of behaviour and a desired outcome, and (wrongly) inferred that the relationship was causal.'

That was how my adolescent mind worked, too. I didn't simply partake in superstitions, I really believed in them. If you exactly replicated the steps that had led to previous success, future success would be inevitable. If you controlled the causal chain, you controlled the outcome. So apparently unconnected events became directly interlinked, fused by my faith in superstition.

At first glance that seems at odds with the fact that I didn't believe in luck. In fact, embracing superstition and rejecting luck are two sides of the same coin. What appealed to me about superstition was the same thing that made me wary of luck: I wanted to be in control. Superstition is what happens when we confuse randomness (which we can't control) with causes (which we can control).

In my case, it eased over time. First, faith in the power of my superstitions inevitably waned with experience. How could it not? Experience has to leave some kind of mark! After all, results vary even when superstitions are constant. Second, part of growing up is recognizing the limitations of your willpower. Accepting that forces exist beyond your control is part of being a well-adjusted adult. Do you want to go through your whole life, like a pigeon at the feeding trough, thinking that you control the destiny of your whole environment by watching *Teletubbies* every day?

I never thought about it at the time, but looking back at my teenage years I can see that my cocky exterior concealed a total control freak. I didn't like to take risks in games I played. And I didn't like to play games I couldn't win. Life took on a binary form: it was either about winning, or about not taking part. Everything in the middle unsettled me.

I was certainly good at the game of winning. In terms of runs scored and matches won, in terms of prizes and 'A' grades, I was very successful. But from another perspective, it's harder to say. Success and failure is one axis; open and closed is another. I was closed to risk and uncertainty, distrustful of unforeseen forks in the road, contemptuous of luck. I was as bad at being open to new things as I was successful at winning clearly defined games that I'd already learnt. Perhaps that is no success at all.

What changed me? Luck, I think. It took me until I was thirty to learn about luck and to realize it was the most important idea I'd ever confronted. This book is about that journey.

2

The silver spoon

I

Both my sister and I went to the local state primary school in north Tonbridge in Kent. It could scarcely have been a more typical or unflashy suburb. The school fence is directly opposite the entrance to the Saturday market, the kind of market that you find in just about every small town in England. It's the same fayre everywhere: with the smell of frying onions from the burger van in your nostrils, you can buy dodgy satellite dishes (they'd just been invented) for £50, or – more at my end of the market when I was at school – three fake 'Fruit of the Loom' T-shirts for a fiver.

The primary school was, and still is, a good school, but with some undeniable drawbacks. When I was there in the early 1980s, some classrooms had been built as temporary buildings but had ended up being retained as full-time classrooms. These caravan-style trailers, standing on bricked-up stilts, stood next to the playground, reminders that the money had dried up.

There were some playing fields at the back of the school, but we didn't use them much. A little bit of rounders in summer, an occasional football match, a yearly athletics competition. There was a weekly PE class in the assembly hall. Taken together, it was probably no worse than the average sporting education in a 1980s primary school, perhaps even a little better.

There were no matches against other schools, not one. And I never picked up a cricket bat at primary school. The most competitive activity I engaged in was playing marbles in the playground. At marbles I was pretty effective, though I don't know how much of that was down to the fact that I was quite an accomplished cheat. (The equation was simple: you risked your single marble by throwing it at the banker, whose pyramid of marbles was yours for the taking if you could hit it. But if you missed, he pocketed the marble you'd just thrown and added it to his bank reserves. I used to creep forward illegally, improving my chances of a direct hit and a bag full of winnings.)

I'm not sure how we were supposed to develop a serious passion for sport. Not only was there little provision within the school, we were never encouraged to join a sports club outside school. Most kids played no sport at all. At home I was playing sport non-stop – not only with my parents, but also against my sister. So I assumed I was a better sportsman than everyone else at school because I cared and knew more about it. But when it came to the (very) occasional formal race or competition, I usually got a nasty shock. I was distinctly average.

For the summer Sports Day, the school would measure out a crudely marked racing track on the grass. Sports Day was tough for me. I'd have to watch kids who'd never been taught to run or encouraged to focus on sport cruise past me as though I was standing still. For all my certainty that I was going to be a great sportsman, in terms of athletic ability I was in the middle of the class – if, that is, there'd been any athletics classes.

Though I was always the more focused about sport, it was my elder sister Becky, not me, who was the better runner and swimmer. She was also fiercely competitive. As she was three and a half years older than me, the result was a lot of defeats for her younger brother. I would lose at every game we played – from Monopoly to Swingball.

For those who haven't played it, Swingball simulates a tennis match, only the ball is attached to a rope which winds around a post. The two players stand on opposite sides of the post, trying to hit the ball so fast that their rival cannot hit it back in their direction. Each time one player misses a shot, the rope winds around the post, registering a 'click'. Once five clicks have been registered by the dominant player, the game is won.

My sister's insight was that a ball attached to a rope deviates in flight according to the trajectory with which it leaves your own racket. Hit the ball upwards, and it will reach your opponent by his ankles. Hit it downwards, and he'll have to jump up to reach. Your opponent receives an exact mirror image of the direction in which you hit the ball. You guessed it. Becky repeatedly hit it down, so that her much shorter little brother couldn't jump high enough to hit the ball at all. So a typical game went something like this:

Whack (her)

Miss (me)

Click (the Swingball post)

Whack (her)

Miss (me)

Click (the Swingball post)

Whack (her)

Miss (me)

Click (the Swingball post)

Whack (her)

Miss (me)

Click (the Swingball post)

Whack (her)

Miss (me)

Final winning click (the Swingball post)

Total time of contest: 6½ seconds.

'That's it! I win! I'm the champion! You're hopeless! You lose! Another game? Come on, let's try again. Can't get any worse . . .'

This sequence was repeated until tea-time. In fact, it was repeated almost until I got taller than her.

My sister would even be picked ahead of me when we played beach cricket with strangers on holidays in Cornwall or South Wales. After the casual preliminary knock-about, when the serious stuff began, and two captains were nominated to pick their team, it was always Becky who was chosen before me. Where I was stylish, she just got the job done. I had the perfect batting stance and tried to bat like Geoff Boycott. She held the bat like a club and hit the ball into the sea and ran twelve while some hapless non-swimming fielder risked his life to retrieve it. Stop the game? You must be joking. She'd run up and down between those lines in the sand until the game was as good as won, glancing occasionally over her shoulder to check that the yellow tennis ball was still bobbing up and down on the surf.

She wasn't just older, she was seriously good. Obviously, at the time, getting whipped by my sister wasn't much fun. But it definitely honed my competitiveness. In my last book, I thanked Becky for her unforgiving tactics. The rest of life, even professional sport, was relatively uncompetitive compared to growing up alongside my sister.

It was typically self-absorbed of me, when I was still a cricketer, to be thinking about how she had helped *me*. The more interesting question, I can see now, is what happened to *her*? What happened to the sporting development of my talented and fiercely competitive big sister?

That story starts with schools. At secondary level, our educational paths diverged. She went to the state grammar school (Kent is one of the few places that still has grammars). I went to the independent school. Why the apparently unjust discrepancy? It was decided by pure chance and opportunity. My dad taught at the independent school, which was boys only, and the fees were effectively waived for the teachers' sons. My parents couldn't afford to send either of us to an equivalent fee-paying school, so our schooling was essentially determined by our sex. If Dad had taught at an independent girls' school, my sister would have been privately educated and I'd have gone to the local grammar. (I sat and passed the eleven-plus exam in case Dad did change the school he taught at.) As it was, he stayed put. I was lucky enough to get an independent education as good as free. My sister didn't.

As you can imagine, this discrepancy between the son and the daughter has not gone unremarked upon during family conversations over the last twenty years. The nub of the issue from my sister's perspective is not academic. Her grammar school was full of clever girls. She was one of them, and went on to study English at Oxford. Where she felt let down was in the rest of her education – the drama, the music and, especially, the sport. Becky dropped out of competitive sport as soon as she could. The brilliantly competitive eleven-year-old played no organized sport for the next two decades. Once she stopped playing sport at school, she stopped playing sport anywhere.

She would be the first to admit that school doesn't explain the whole story. Her school did offer some opportunities to play competitive sport that she could have signed up for. But she is right that the comparison between her school sport and my school sport was extremely marked.

We had a 25-metre indoor heated swimming pool (now

upgraded to a superlative Olympic version with accompanying gym and exercise rooms). We had twelve rugby pitches, each tended to perfection and cut in geometric stripes. We had two hockey AstroTurfs that doubled up as twenty-one tennis courts. We had a rackets court. We had seven fives courts. We had four squash courts. We had an Olympic-standard running track. We had more cricket nets – ten artificial ones, and ten grass ones – than any professional team I ever played for. And the quality of the 1st XI cricket pitch was astonishing. Lord's, the most famous ground in the world, has the smoothest outfield I ever fielded on. The *second* best is my school ground.

Think about that for a moment. In thirteen years as a professional cricketer – despite playing in India, Australia, South Africa and Malaysia – I only experienced one outfield better than my *school* pitch. Playing a 1st team cricket match at my school was like playing football at Anfield. That's how good the facilities were. The only problem with sport at my school was the recurrent problem with exceptional educational privilege: how could things possibly get better after you left? From my sister's point of view, the comparative prospect of scraping her knees on the state school Tarmac netball court didn't really appeal.

In a sense, my sister and I were part of an accidental educational experiment. Take two children with similar genes and similar talent: send one to a state school and the other to an independent school. What happened to my sister's sporting experience was that she ran out of opportunities – not completely, but significantly. What happened to my sporting experience was that I received the best sporting education money can buy. I played cricket for England. She didn't play for any team in any sport ever again.

II

The role of luck in the making of sports stars has become a hot topic. The physicist John Wesson has shown that the probability of becoming a Premiership footballer is twice as high for boys born in the autumn as for those born in the summer. The English academic year runs from September to July, so in terms of physical development autumn babies are ahead.

It is called 'accumulative advantage'. The slightly stronger and bigger sporting child is singled out for extra coaching and more attention. New opportunities are extended to the high achiever and denied to the young struggler. These early advantages of luck harden into a lasting divergence.

Malcolm Gladwell popularized the idea in *Outliers*. In Canada, 40 per cent of professional hockey players are born between January and March, 30 per cent between April and June, 20 per cent between July and September, and 10 per cent between October and December. It's become known as the 'January effect'.

But before parents desperate to have superstar children dedicate their lives to attempting conception at the 'right' time of the academic year, there are other chance factors that influence sporting development. A recent study at Queen's University in Canada explored the backgrounds of over 2,000 American professional athletes.

They made the startling discovery that an unignorably high proportion of star athletes come from small towns. Just over half the American population lives in cities with populations above half a million people. And yet these big cities only produce 13 per cent of professional hockey players, 29 per cent of NBA players, 15 per cent of Major League baseball players and 13 per cent of pro golfers. There is a huge bias towards smaller cities. Eighty-five per cent of elite baseball players come from 48 per cent of the population. In other words, for two equally talented players, the one from a small town is six times more likely to get to the top than the player from the big city.

Perhaps the explanation is nothing more complicated than that smaller towns (like the one where I grew up) provide more space for kids to run around and play sports. But Sian Beilock, a psychologist at the University of Chicago, has a subtler theory. She believes that the advantage of small towns is that they are *less* competitive. Because there are fewer players competing to get into local teams, children in smaller cities get to sample many different sports. As a result, they don't specialize too early.

The result is that talented sports kids are less likely to suffer from physical or psychological burn-out. They retain a healthier balance by playing lots of games. And they avoid repetitive strain injuries that are increasingly affecting children forced into insane degrees of practice by over-ambitious parents. It's common for an American ten-year-old baseball pitcher to need tendon replacement surgery; a few years ago, such physical burn-out was known only among college stars and professionals. In other words, making kids specialize too early carries enormous risks. (I think I suffered from over-specialization, as we'll see later, though it was my own fault, not that of my resolutely unpushy parents.)

Beilock's findings are a welcome and civilizing corrective. Conventional wisdom assumes that would-be champions must give up normal life in early childhood and dedicate their whole existence to one narrow activity. We might call this the 'Tiger Woods fallacy': believing that the only way to become great is to pursue single-minded dedication to one game from the age of three.

The January effect and the small-town bias have become quite famous studies of luck in sporting sociology. But each is rather different from the luck I am describing here, the good fortune of attending a private school. There is a big difference between genuinely arbitrary luck (identified by Beilock and Gladwell) and luck that is economically predetermined.

That two children's sporting prospects – mine and my sister's, for example – significantly diverge because of their schools is about non-random luck. It's about a weighting of opportunity. It's about privilege. It opens up a debate about justice and fairness. It gets to the heart of what we really mean when we examine whether life is a level playing field. It is as uncomfortable as the January effect is amusing.

III

Thirteen cricketers represented England on the tour to Pakistan in 1987/8. Twelve of them were educated at state schools; only one had been at a private school. Now roll the clock on twenty-three years. The England team that beat India at Lord's in 2011 consisted of eight privately educated players, and three state-educated ones. In 1987, then, 92 per cent were state educated. That almost exactly mirrors British society as a whole: 93 per cent state educated and 7 per cent privately educated. By contrast, the England team of 2011 had 27 per cent state-educated players and 73 per cent privately educated ones.

It is the same in rugby union. At the 1987 World Cup, sixteen of the twenty-six (or 62 per cent) had attended state schools. By 2007, eight of the twenty were state educated (or 36 per cent).

If you think cricket and rugby are unrepresentative, let's look at British Olympians. At the 1984 Los Angeles Olympics, six of the nine British gold medallists had their education funded by the state. But in 2008 only half the gold medallists went to state schools. And it's not just gold medals: the proportion of British medallists who are privately educated has grown steadily to about 45 per cent.

The trend is the same in cricket, in rugby, in Olympic sports. There are now more elite sportsmen who went to secondary schools like mine, and fewer players who went to schools like my sister's.

There are two obvious objections to my study. First, where is football? Why have I not compared a 1980s England football team with a late 2000s one? The answer is that private schools rarely focus on football. As a result, the absence of private schoolboys in top-flight English football has been a constant. Frank Lampard, who went to Brentwood, is one of a tiny number. Arsenal's historian estimated that just one private schoolboy had played for the club in the last forty years. So football, despite being the country's most popular sport, doesn't tell us very much about social mobility. It shows a flat line, not a trend.

Second, perhaps my small sample of cricket, rugby and Olympic teams is misleading. What if those particular sides from the 1980s and the late 2000s were untypical?

So let's broaden the search to include all England teams. We know the educational backgrounds of the vast majority of England rugby players since the first international in 1871. What do we learn about these 800 or so players? It is no surprise that an originally amateur sport like rugby was at first overwhelmingly dominated by the private schools. But in the 1950s, 1960s and 1970s, the proportion of state-educated players grows steadily, peaking in the mid-1980s. In fact, about two-thirds of those selected between 1981 and 1990 were state educated. But that trend reverses in the 1990s and

2000s. If you plot the results as a graph, you get the pattern shown in Figure 1.

Figure 1

Percentage of England Rugby Union Internationals Educated at State Schools, Selected Years 1871–2009

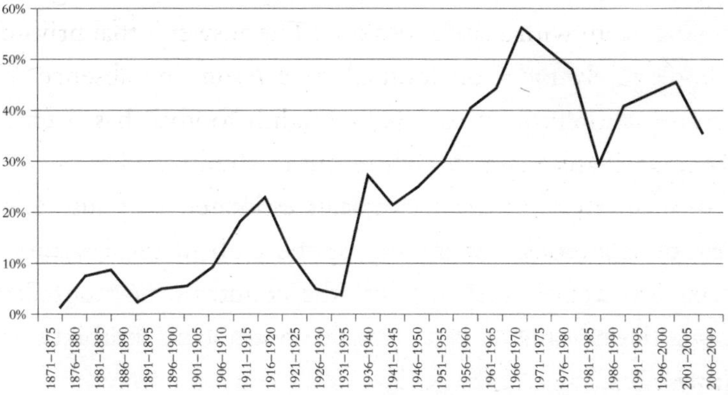

Note: No data for years 1915–19 or 1941–45. Data displayed as continuous line graph to show the general trend over time.
Sources: Tony Collins, *A Social History of English Rugby Union* (Routledge, 2009), author's calculations.

Cricket tells a similar story, only with a different starting point. Historically, cricket was a more cross-class sport than rugby, with a less marked private-school orientation than rugby. Whatever Americans may imagine about country houses and cream teas, cricket was never traditionally an elitist sport.

But it is becoming one. Though less extreme, cricket's graph reveals a similar post-war trend to rugby's. The proportion of state-educated players increased steadily in the 1950, 1960s and 1970s. It peaked in the 1980s, before reversing in the 1990s and 2000s. Seven per cent of the population is privately educated; 93 per cent of the population is state educated. And yet the 7 per cent contributes over two thirds of the players in the current England cricket team. In other words, being state educated makes it about twenty times less likely that you will play for England. That really is a waste of talent.

IV

One of the unchallenged narratives during my career in cricket was that the game was 'moving on' from the days of class and privilege. When I'd just started out at Kent, the captaincy became vacant, and the leading candidate was a privately educated player. One of the other players explained to me that this man 'couldn't possibly get the job' because Kent had 'moved on from being captained by that kind of player'. What he meant was that, once, privately educated players had become captain by right, by default. Now, in the meritocratic world of modern cricket, it was practically inconceivable that a toff could take the reins.

It's the kind of comment I heard – and read – throughout my career. Sometimes I found to my surprise that it was my background about which assumptions were being made. Before the captaincy of an England 'A' tour was announced, one leading cricket journalist suggested I was the default choice as captain only because I had 'a Cambridge Blue and a decent cut of jib'. The heavy implication was that cricket should 'move on' from such snobbish preconceptions about leadership and that the selectors should choose someone else. They did. But they could only manage another player who'd been educated at private school.

Even the unflashy Andrew Strauss, of Radley College and Durham University, was made to wait an awfully long time to become England captain. I think there was a splash of inverted snobbery that held him back. After all, cricket teams had 'moved on' from needing to be captained by a player from 'the right background'.

Cricket was 'moving on'. But not in the way everyone assumed. As state schools have stopped playing cricket, the social composition of English cricket has narrowed. It is not the leaders who have changed, it is the whole cohort – and in the opposite direction from the presumptions of conventional wisdom.

The fact that England's Test one-day and Twenty20 captains – Andrew Strauss, Alastair Cook and Stuart Broad – attended fee-paying schools is not symptomatic of a class conspiracy within the corridors of power. It's a reflection of the fact that over half the team comes from 7 per cent of the population. Most of the 93 per cent never get the opportunity to play cricket at all. When Chance to Shine was launched in 2005, a charity that tries to redress the gulf in cricketing opportunities between private and state schools, it calculated that fewer than 10 per cent of state schools offered any meaningful cricket.

It is a seriously misleading tendency to assume that the

advantages of class and money are being swept away. When Danny Cipriani, the brilliantly talented England fly half, placed the rugby ball on his kicking tee before his first kick at goal early in his full England debut in March 2008, the television commentator chose this moment to discuss Cipriani's class background rather than his rugby skills.

'His mum was a cab driver,' the commentator enlightened us, before going on to say that this fact disproved the idea that rugby is a posh game only for toffs. It was said with a great sense of authorial approval, as though this single nugget of parental information provided the clinching evidence that rugby union – for so long the bastion of amateur values and the public school ethos – had finally grown up. The implication was clear: rugby had changed.

In the same vein, a highly respected sportswriter at the *Guardian* announced that the 2007 England rugby team represented a new, better, fairer kind of Britain. On the eve of the 2007 Rugby World Cup final, he celebrated an age of meritocracy in English rugby:

> When France won football's World Cup in 1998, their players were acclaimed for providing a snapshot of their country's multi-cultural make-up ... This was a France dreamed of by optimists. Something similar can be said, curiously enough, of England's rugby team. If this World Cup can achieve anything beyond the handing out of medals to the winners, it will be to take the wrecking ball to a stereotype of the game's ambience [i.e. wealth and privilege] that may once

have contained a certain truth but is now, as a working definition, utterly obsolete.

In truth, fourteen of the England rugby squad that played
in the 2007 World Cup final were privately educated. The gap
between myth and reality is widening as fast as the gap
between haves and have-nots. (Cipriani, by the way, went to
a private school.)

V

Does sport reflect the rest of Britain? Are we stuck using the
rhetoric of meritocracy in an increasingly unmeritocratic
society? That was the question the broadcaster and journalist
Andrew Neil set himself for a 2011 BBC documentary. Neil
was educated at a selective state school in the 1960s, an
education that has served him well. But he now asked if
'someone from my ordinary background could still enjoy the
same opportunities I had'. Was a new generation of people
like Andrew Neil coming through, or had politics 'again
become the preserve of the privileged'?

First Neil described the meritocracy he had benefited
from. In his version, the watershed came in 1964 when the
state-educated Harold Wilson was elected Prime Minister.
From 1964 to 1997, the office of Prime Minister was exclu-
sively filled by politicians who had been educated at state
schools: Harold Wilson, Ted Heath, Jim Callaghan, Margaret

Thatcher and John Major. (In cricket, 1966 began a state-school era of captains with Brian Close and then Ray Illingworth.)

The Prime Ministerial sequence ended with Tony Blair in 1997, and then David Cameron (briefly interrupted by the state-educated Gordon Brown). Neil added:

> In supposedly modern, meritocratic 21st century Britain, the Prime Minister, the Deputy Prime Minister, the Leader of the opposition, the Chancellor and the shadow Chancellor all went to Oxbridge, three of the five did the same degree and all were privately educated bar one [Ed Miliband]. More men from a single Oxford college – Magdalen – sit around the Cabinet table than women of any background.

He argued that the shift is representative. The composition of the House of Commons is also moving in the same direction. More than a third of the House elected in 2010 is privately educated, three percentage points more than that elected in 2005, reversing a downward trend established over several generations. Neil went on to suggest that the narrowing political elite reflected the rest of society: 'Despite the recent massive investment in schools, the attainment gap between state and private is bigger only in Turkey ... Almost a third of public-school pupils get at least three A-levels at grade A, versus 7.5 per cent of comprehensive pupils, a gap that has doubled since 1998.'

The New Labour government made increasing meritocracy one of its catchphrases. In his speech at the 1999 Labour Party conference, Tony Blair stated that broadening opportunity was his most cherished ideal: 'But the part [of my job] that matters most to me is getting my sleeves rolled up and pushing through the changes to our country that will give to others by right what I achieved by good fortune.'

But when the former Labour minister Alan Milburn chaired a panel in 2009 to examine social mobility, he agreed with Andrew Neil's unmeritocratic findings. Some 75 per cent of judges, 70 per cent of finance directors, 54 per cent of leading journalists, 45 per cent of top civil servants and 32 per cent of MPs had attended private schools. Milburn concluded: 'The UK's professions have become more, not less, socially exclusive over time ... Children born – as I was – in 1958 were far less dependent on the economic status of their parents than those born in later years. Birth not worth has become more key to life chances.'

Milburn's findings echo the famous 2005 social-mobility study by the Sutton Trust. It compared the cohort of men born in 1958 with the cohort born in 1970. The question here is how much the prosperity of your family influences your prospects of making money yourself. In a highly mobile society, the influence of family wealth on the next generation is slight. In less mobile societies, the influence is strong.

Though some have challenged its conclusions, the Sutton Trust report found that the chances of making it from the bottom quartile to the top quartile were *better* for the 1958 cohort than for the 1970 cohort. In other words, Britain had become more governed by privilege, not less. When I read that Sutton Trust report, I realized that the two generations it compared – that born in 1958 and that born in 1970 – were roughly contemporaneous with the two generations I compared in my study of the England sporting teams. My tiny study follows the same pattern as their far broader one. We have become less a meritocracy, more a fortunocracy.

Ironically, just as real meritocracy appears to be heading into reverse, phoney meritocracy is ubiquitous: mockney accents, dumbing down, pressing meritocratic buttons, covering your privileged tracks. It is passed off as modesty, as the everyman touch. In fact, it is quite the opposite. Pretending to have fewer advantages than you did is not only a form of deceit. It is also a form of conceit. It is an attempt to deny your good luck in order to claim more credit for yourself. Dickens lampooned such self-aggrandizement in his satirical attacks on Mr Bounderby in *Hard Times*. Bounderby was a self-styled self-made man. Only he wasn't self-made. Bounderby was born with a silver spoon in his mouth. He was just too arrogant to admit it.

VI

Who am I to talk about meritocracy and education? Unlike Andrew Neil, who has the legitimacy of having gone to a state school, I am a product of a (largely) private education.

That is exactly the point. One of the biggest honours of my life was playing cricket for England in 2003. My selection was not inevitable, like Kevin Pietersen's, because he was so much better and more naturally talented than everyone else. I was a marginal pick. I needed every leg-up I could get along the way.

It's not the kind of question you reflect on when you're still a player. When I was still competing, I naturally didn't think too much about how I might never have been selected. I was focused on getting back into the England team, not dreaming up what-ifs in which I had never got there in the first place. But now, safely retired, I no longer have to worry about uncomfortable logic or painful truths. So I choose my words carefully and base them on empirical evidence. If better sporting education was freely available to all young people in England, as it was to me, I probably wouldn't have played for England. Someone with more innate talent would have taken my place. They didn't. Lucky for me. Not so lucky for England.

3

When we abolished luck

Books about luck often rely on experimental sociology. I could have tossed 10,000 coins to observe a random sequence of heads and tails. Or flipped 500 slices of buttered toast to see if Murphy's Law (anything that can go wrong *will* go wrong) held up to the rigours of empirical research. Or perhaps I could have pursued an academic sociology experiment in which, let's say, 200 Nevadans were asked if they felt lucky before being lowered to the bottom of the Grand Canyon and told to find a way back to the top. I could then write an academic paper on whether Marlon Brando, in *A Streetcar Named Desire*, was right when he said that 'Luck is believing you're lucky.'

Then I realized I'd already conducted a sociological experiment about luck. Only I hadn't conducted it with a neutral academic perspective. I'd been on the inside as one of the guinea pigs. I'd been the subject of the experiment, not the researcher. It all flooded back to me. As a twenty-one-year-old, I'd been exposed to social conditions that are usually reserved only for tribesmen among the Azande and the Dobuan (we'll come to them later). A decade before I'd even considered writing this book, I'd lived in a community that didn't have access to the concept of luck.

It was the year I became a full-time professional cricketer with Kent County Cricket Club in 1999. Coincidentally, Kent was beginning a new push to become a great team. We were given ring-binders full of documents headed 'Kent Cricket – World Class'. This was a new era. The age of ultra-professionalism had arrived. And professionalism, of course, above all demands control. No longer would 'anything be left to chance' (chance was an awful relic of amateurism). There would be specialists for everything – physiologists, psychologists, nutritionists, optometrists. One player quipped that the only -ologists not represented were gynaecologists.

We also spent a great deal of time discussing how we would play, even how we would live. For a twenty-one-year-old cricketer, just turning pro, it proved a bizarre introduction to the hardened world of professional sport. It was like living through an experiment in social engineering. The team's previous problems and differences would be erased. A *blank sheet of paper*, the 'team builder' kept saying, *starting from zero*.

I will never forget that first week as a professional sportsman. Our home ground in Canterbury basked in warm and sunny March weather, but the team did not use the perfect practice conditions to hone our batting and bowling skills. Instead, we were confined in a room for three days to decide on the precise wording for a team 'Core Covenant'.

This team constitution was intended to revolutionize us into an unstoppable professional outfit. Noble sentiments coexisted with practical commands. The Core Covenant included a 'pledge' (after all, this was the high point of New Labour) to catch fifty extra practice catches every day. Come what may – even after a close game, even if we were exhausted, even if it was snowing – we would catch fifty extra catches. A small voice of reason asked if we wouldn't simply break more fingers? Maybe we *ought* – no, *had* – to break a few fingers, the coach replied.

I feel guilty, as I write this, to be raking over the history of that bizarre month in 1999. I can see now that both the new coach and the new captain were astonishingly committed leaders and good people. I do not mean to mock their idealism, not least because I believed in their ambition more than most. Perhaps the problem was partly on my side. Because I was unusually idealistic and analytical, I may have taken the whole thing more seriously than I should have. When you are desperate to succeed, you are especially vulnerable to utopian thinking.

At one Core Covenant meeting, we were all asked to say what we wanted to change about the team. One senior player brought up the issue of luck. 'What really annoys me is when a batsman gets out and the rest of us say, "Bad luck". That's soft. If you're out, it's not unlucky. We're just creating an excuse.' I know what he meant. A team can be too tolerant of using luck as an excuse. Many dismissals, of course, are entirely caused by error on the part of the batsman and luck does indeed have nothing to do with them. I think the senior player was trying to remind us to be tough on ourselves rather than always rushing to blame bad luck. In a different context, the remark would have been nothing more than a throwaway comment.

But in the environment of 1999, the year of cricketing utopia, in the spirit of starting from zero, in our brave new dawn, this throwaway line about luck was seized upon as revealed truth. There would be no more 'bad lucks', not one, not ever. Abolishing luck slotted in nicely as a central plank of our philosophy.

The 'no luck' principle was written into the Core Covenant and passed into law. The concept was banned. We would no longer make such lame excuses. Luck belonged to the bad old days before the Core Covenant.

So 1999 – even the year had a utopian ring – was to be *a season without luck*. It had been summarily abolished. Allowing for the existence of luck was for our weak-willed rival teams. We knew better. Instead of luck, we chose unflinching honesty and searing self-criticism. Luck was for cowards.

Once the Covenant's other main articles (mostly abstract nouns) and dozens of sub-headings were agreed, we all signed the master document, like the barons at Magna Carta. Individual laminated print-offs were distributed for us to pin inside our kit bags, a reminder of the professional code of conduct that we would live by. The Core Convenant had passed into law.

I wish I could claim, writing this over a decade later, that I'd seen through the Core Covenant all along. But it would not be true. I signed up to the ideology. The idea of banishing luck – and other forms of human frailty – appealed to the ultra-rationalist in me.

But it had some bizarre effects. None of us had anticipated how luck was bound up with the way we talked and thought about the game. Cricketers usually say 'Good luck' to the new batsman when it is his turn to bat. They also often, but not always, say 'Bad luck' when he is out. It is not always meant literally. Sometimes, inevitably, luck does indeed have nothing to do with it, but that had always been implicitly understood. Saying 'Bad luck' could mean several things. Sometimes it meant 'That really was bad luck'; other days it was just a way of softening the blow for someone who felt distraught.

The season finally began with our match against Middlesex at Lord's. After writing the Core Covenant during bright sunshine, the rest of spring had been blighted by persistent rain – not a question of bad luck, obviously – and we arrived at Lord's under-prepared. The whole team seemed a bit confused, especially me.

Despite that, I was convinced that the first game of the season would be the start of a new era, a world in which mistakes didn't happen. With excuses banished and weakness outlawed, what could stop me from making a massive score?

I visualized a hundred – no, a double hundred. It *had* to be 200. I'd stamp my authority on the season. This was a new start, a new way of thinking and playing.

This grand new beginning turned out to be much less glamorous than I'd imagined. In the first game of the season, played in appalling weather, I didn't bat until about 6 p.m., just before the close of play. As soon as the last Middlesex wicket fell, I charged off the field to get padded up, already breathing heavily with anxiety. I then hurried back on to the pitch, tense and anxious. My kit felt ill-fitting and my mind unsettled.

Meanwhile, the rest of the world was going through the motions. It was a freezing April day, nearly dark, and only a few hardy spectators had stayed to the end of play. The Middlesex fielders had their hands in their pockets. The bowler looked stiff in the freezing cold.

As a matter of fact, he didn't need to be feeling very flexible. I did not present a difficult challenge for him. I felt paralysed by a sense of pressure and every ball bowled at me arrived before I was ready. Instead of my bat hitting the ball, the ball seemed to cannon into the bat when it wanted to. I had no control, no belief, no joy. Worst of all – and I was someone who was thought to have a lot of self-belief – I wasn't sure I even wanted to be out there on the pitch. A part of me just wanted everything to be over, to restart the computer. I was out lamely, LBW for 3.

I would fail many more times over the next ten years as a professional cricketer, but never again like that. I had 'choked', for the first (and last) time in my cricket career. The unusual thing about my choke is that the stakes weren't particularly high. It wasn't a cup final, or my first innings for England (when I would be far less nervous). No, the pressure didn't come from the objective importance of the fixture but from the rarefied environment I'd been living in.

We'd signed up to utopia – a world without excuses, without weakness, without luck – and that gloomy spring day was set in my mind as the foundation stone. Determined to make my first innings the start of a new era, I succeeded only in making cricket even harder.

There was light snow in the London evening air as I hurried off the field after getting out ignominiously. I almost ran into the dressing room, embarrassed and humiliated in a way I'd never known before.

What did everyone say in the dressing room? Not a sound. We daren't use the 'L' word. We'd abolished it.

4

Breaking point

I

I was standing on the most famous cricket pitch in the world with a coin in my hand about to flip it into the late afternoon sunshine. The ground is Lord's, the home of cricket, in St John's Wood, north-west London. It became my home, too, in 2005 when I left Kent to join Middlesex. A few hundred yards away, the Beatles recorded Abbey Road. In fact, Sir Paul McCartney still lives around the corner. Those two facts tell you a lot about how St John's Wood has changed: it used to be ordinary, now it's spectacularly wealthy.

To be honest, I've never fretted much about what to call. It sounds crazy, but some people do. 'Heads never fails . . . Always call tails at the seaside . . .' Even tossing a coin before a cricket match has become swamped with superstition. I knew one captain who privately flipped his own coin on the way out to the official coin toss. If heads won in this trial run, he'd call tails in the real thing. If tails won, he'd call heads. His reasoning, if you can call it that, was that you're less likely to get two tails in a row, right?

It would be easy to mock such an abject failure to understand randomness. But I wasn't much better. Not if you take everything together, all my superstitions and rituals and attempts to control things that, rationally, I knew couldn't be controlled. So I'm not going to lambast the mad captain who didn't understand probability theory.

You would think, given all the sophisticated ways that sport has evolved, that we would have invented a fairer system than a coin toss to determine how the match will begin. Does it matter? Ask Nasser Hussain, the former England captain. He lost fourteen consecutive tosses – the odds against which are 16,384 to 1 – and it didn't help his efforts to turn England into a winning team. Still, he had only himself to blame. He kept calling heads.

As I flip the coin in the air tonight, Mark Pettini, the Essex captain, calls heads, too. It's only while the coin is in flight that you realize the true extent of your helplessness. You've spent days preoccupied with decisions about who to pick, you've obsessed about tactics, talked with coaches and raked over all the statistics. You know that Essex like to bat second, or that 68 per cent of games in June are won by the team that wins the toss. You checked the Met Office website – if there's a chance of rain, you'll definitely want to field first. At every turn, in every minute of strategizing and planning, you hope to gain perhaps a tenth of 1 per cent's advantage – the 'edge', gamblers call it. You also know the other team is doing it, too, but you try to believe you're doing it better.

And yet for all the planning, we hand over to blind chance – or dumb luck, if you prefer – something as serious as *the order in which the match takes place*. What kind of a crazy game is this? Couldn't we find a more rational way of determining things?

The pound coin comes down tails. I've won the toss. We'll field first, thank you, I say, shaking Pettini's hand again. That feels promising. It feels very promising. We have won our last four games, and now – in what I hope will be the fifth – we've already gained a real advantage.

As I walked back to the pavilion, I see fans pouring in through the gates and moving to their seats. There are probably 20,000 people already here. Five wins in a row, how great would that feel? I'm not sure I've ever played in a team that's won five in a row.

Christ, get a grip, man. You've only won the toss.

II

It had been a different, bleaker story five weeks earlier. In the four-day competition, we began the season with two draws and two defeats. In the one-day league, our first six games were evenly split – three wins, three defeats.

It's hard to know exactly what made the season suddenly take off in late May. We won two consecutive four-day games, followed by a one-day match. Three wins in a row is scarcely an epic sequence. But it was definitely a start.

Better still, it was now time to turn to an entirely new competition, the Twenty20 – the most popular and high-profile league in the English season. For some reason, I had a good feeling about the Twenty20. This was highly idiosyncratic of me, I admit. Our first match was at the Rose Bowl against Hampshire, who had all their star players on view. Few pundits gave us any chance of winning the first match, let alone the whole competition.

But the three previous wins seemed to me like the beginning of something bigger, not just a brief upswing within a broader decline. After speaking to the coach and a few senior players, I wrote a very short note that I handed out to all the players before the game against Hampshire. It covered less than one-side of A4 and it was pretty basic, to say the least. But I did predict we would start and end our Twenty20 campaign with wins at the Rose Bowl. In other words – as the Twenty20 final was due to be played at the Rose Bowl in July – I suggested we would win the competition. Most people, admittedly, would have said I was mad. But that's what I honestly believed.

We won the first match at the Rose Bowl. On a personal note, I don't think I ever hit the ball more sweetly than that day. For the team, that was now four wins in a row, and we headed back to Lord's to play Essex believing we could beat anyone.

The pressure was still on, though. That's always the case for a captain, especially at Middlesex. In the last thirteen years, the Middlesex captaincy has changed hands over twenty times. A man who accepts the job of captaining Middlesex is a bit like a woman who agrees to marry Henry VIII. You do so out of hope rather than rational expectations. In fact, Middlesex has been even more prolific at dispensing with captains than Henry was at rattling through wives.

All this I knew before accepting the job. If I had made a cool calculation of the odds, I wouldn't have taken it. No one would. So why did I? Because every captain thinks it will be different this time. We discount the odds and spin the wheel, believing that history won't repeat itself yet again.

III

For once, on 12 June 2008, as I flipped the coin with Mark Pettini in front of a full house at Lord's, the odds had rarely looked better. We had players in form, a game plan that we believed in, and serious momentum in our favour. The sun was shining on Middlesex cricket, in every sense, for the first time in a long while.

It's a funny feeling when everything goes right. A part of you distrusts it, as though there's something you're not quite getting, a glitch in the small print of the deal that you're not clever enough to see. That's what it felt like when Middlesex fielded first against Essex on 12 June.

What Essex score would I have settled for before we took the field? 160? Definitely. 170? Very winnable. 180? Given our form, I'd have still been optimistic about chasing that total down.

Instead, we bowled out Essex for 115. It was a terrific performance. Captaincy – I can say this now, safely retired and released from the burdens of superstition – seemed easy that day. It was as though we were being drawn towards victory by a providential force. I kept changing the bowling and the bowlers kept bowling perfectly. The ball seemed to be magnetically drawn to the fielders. And we held all our catches as though there was glue in our hands. I've never enjoyed captaining a fielding performance as much as that day at Lord's. It felt as though we *couldn't* lose, even if we'd tried.

When our fast bowler Dirk Nannes took a brilliant catch over his shoulder while running backwards, he shrugged and laughed, 'Never thought I was catching it, to be honest!' When you're winning and playing well and having fun, you can afford to be honest about brief moments of doubt. Confidence was so high that we were catching balls we didn't even think we'd catch.

The atmosphere in the dressing room between innings was very relaxed. We'd done the difficult part. Chasing 115 shouldn't be hard. I don't think I even said anything to the team before we went out to bat. The task at hand seemed self-explanatory.

I was opening the batting with Andrew Strauss. We walked

out through the Long Room, as you always do at Lord's. It's about thirty paces from the swing door at the back of the Long Room to the steps on to the field. Our studs were muffled on the expensive flooring, as stern Victorian faces looked down on us from the portraits hanging on the walls above, and polite applause rippled through the room.

Do you ever get used to walking on to a modern professional sports field through a spectacular Victorian ballroom? Yes and no is the honest answer. Yes, you become inured against misplaced elation – batting is a calm business, after all. But, no, you do not tire of it or take it for granted. A small part of your soul secretly sings, each and every time, as you walk through the Long Room and on to the billiard-table-smooth turf of Lord's. How could it not?

'Cricket is greater than sex,' said Harold Pinter, 'though sex isn't too bad either.' As the finest cricket ground in the world, Lord's is pretty damn sexy.

Our innings started well in terms of runs coming easily, but I wasn't batting very well. Perhaps it was a touch of complacency. After a few mishits and mishaps, I gave myself 'the chat'. I wonder if every batsman has a version of the chat, or if it's just me. Anyway, mine goes something like this:

'Fucking wake up! What are you doing out here? What do you think this is? A piece of cake? Yes, you're feeling good. That's not an invitation to be complacent. How can you not have learnt that after all these years? How many times have you tried 100 per cent and been unlucky or outplayed and had to wait for *weeks* until you felt good again? You know how capricious form is. So why are you so careless about it? If you're feeling confident, show some bloody respect for the game and switch on. Don't just cruise as though you don't have to really engage your full attention.'

I've edited out most of the swear words. In my private voice, there are many more, I'm afraid. Only two things made me furious with myself. The first was complacency. The second was getting ahead of myself – catching myself thinking, 'It will feel so sweet when I get to a hundred.' Then I'd really let loose against the ill-disciplined part of my mind.

Things got better after the chat. I moved my feet a bit quicker. I had more purpose and energy at the crease. And we were winning. Easily. Yes, we had suffered a setback when Strauss was out for 11. It was 22 for 1, and 94 runs still needed for victory. But Strauss's departure brought in Eoin Morgan, the freakishly talented Irishman who hits the ball harder with less effort than anyone I've ever seen.

Those who deny the existence of natural talent must have a hard job explaining Eoin Morgan. He's not especially big. He does not have a very high back-lift. He doesn't swing himself off his feet. Neither brute force nor the physics of movement quite explains it. The ball arrives, the bat descends and with the sweetest of noises and the minimum of effort – *crack!* – it whistles off Morgan's bat like a bullet leaving a rifle. Some people say it's all practice, hitting the ball like that. Well, they can believe that if they want to.

Morgan's batting reminds me of that speech in Tom Stoppard's play *The Real Thing*:

This [cricket bat] here, which looks like a wooden club, is actually several pieces of particular wood cunningly put together in a certain way so that the whole thing is sprung, like a dance floor. It's for hitting cricket balls with. If you get it right, the cricket ball will travel two hundred yards in four seconds, and all you've done is give it a knock like knocking the top off a bottle of stout, and it makes a noise like a trout taking a fly . . .

What we're trying to do is write cricket bats, so that when we throw up an idea and give it a little knock it might . . . travel . . .

Of course, as Stoppard well knows, it's not only about the bat. It's the batsman, too. When Morgan hits the ball, it travels. Like when Stoppard writes. That's not all practice, either. It's talent.

I'm not in the Morgan category. I did, however, start to time the ball better at Lord's that evening. Perhaps the chat had helped. The ball was starting to 'travel', as Stoppard puts it. But I did allow myself one brief glance around the ground. The rain had missed us and the clouds burned away. Lord's never looks better than in high summer, in the soft yellows of a late-afternoon sun. The grandstand was casting long shadows over perfectly tended grass. The turrets of the red-brick pavilion were turning rusty orange in the fading light.

There was warmth in the crowd, as well as in the air. They, like us, knew we were winning. It was one of those rare run-chases that would not have a nervous collapse or even an anxious chapter. After all we had been through – the team, the fans, and, indeed, the captain – this was one to enjoy.

With the Pakistani leg-spinner Danish Kaneria bowling, I hit a two into the outfield. I ran the twenty yards from the batting crease at the Pavilion end to the batting crease at the famous Nursery end. I slowed down, extended my bat in my right hand and touched it over the crease. It is a subconscious series of actions for any professional batsman. How many times do we do it in a career, in a lifetime? We score perhaps 100,000 runs, all taken together, in every game of cricket, from childhood to the end, over the course of a cricketing life. So we touch down in the crease and turn for the second run tens of thousands of times.

This day was no different. There was no pressure from the fielder. It was easy, routine, run of the mill. So I pushed off my left foot, as I turned back towards the Pavilion. There was a cracking noise, and I found myself crumpled in a heap on the ground. I tried to stand up. I needed to run to the other end. But I couldn't stand. I could only sit on my back-side and I shouted at Eoin Morgan to go back to his end. So we'd lost one run – it should have been two, but instead we only got one. We'd make up that lost run in no time, I thought. This was too good a day for the loss of one solitary run to hurt us.

I pushed up again. And fell down again. Someone in the crowd laughed, as though I was a clown who'd lost his balance.

IV

It took what seemed like an embarrassingly long time for me to get up. I could stand, eventually, but I couldn't run.

We're lucky in cricket, if lucky is the right word, that the game makes provision for such injuries. One of the batsmen who has already been dismissed can run for the injured player. The injured batter can stay on the pitch and hit the ball, but someone else does the running for him. This meant that Andrew Strauss had to put down his coffee in the dressing room, strap his pads and gloves back on, and return to the pitch as my runner.

I'm not very good at gauging pain. In advance, I'm a bit of a wimp about discomfort – trips to the dentist, injections, fitness tests. When I know that pain is inevitably around the corner, I dread it. But when pain just happens to me, without warning, I don't seem to process it properly. Maybe it is all a case of childhood conditioning. My dad was a gentle father in lots of ways, but not about injuries. When I'd fall off the climbing frame as a kid, he'd stand over me and look in my eyes and say the same thing every time, 'Don't cry. Just don't cry.' I think he felt his own parents had been too easily worried about his health, that they'd smothered him with concern, to his own detriment. He'd reacted against their softness. With me, it was always, 'Don't feel it. It doesn't hurt. Don't allow yourself to show any pain.'

He was the same about illness. He missed scarcely a day of work in forty years. He didn't acknowledge illness; it was like a category error. He expected the same from me. If I said I was ill to my mum on a school morning, Dad would come into my bedroom, stand by the door, with the whole distance of the room between him and me, not even getting closer to look carefully, and say, 'You're fine. Go to school.' It ran against his true character in many ways, that stern streak. But it left a deep impression on me.

So how injured did I think I was at Lord's that day? I didn't know. I wasn't thinking clearly. Why? Because I'm not good at gauging pain. Because I hadn't been injured for ten years (I broke my finger playing against South Africa as a twenty-year-old, but since then I hadn't missed a game through injury), so I had nothing similar to compare it to. Because my blood was up and we were winning and Middlesex were on a roll and this was destined to be another great day. Because the odds, for once, were stacked in our favour. Because the tide had turned. Because fate was smiling on us. Because we were having the success we deserved. Because life was too good to feel much pain. Because this streak couldn't be threatened.

It just couldn't. Not now. Not after all that.

V

At the time, I can see it was quite comic. In retrospect, it isn't so funny. When a batter has a runner, farce is always around the corner. There are too many voices, too many minds, too much confusion. It often ends in a run-out, with everyone stranded at one end, with the injured player forgetting he's supposed to stay anchored in his crease and the runner looking baffled and embarrassed. Having a runner is an accident – another accident – waiting to happen.

This time, though, things went reasonably smoothly. Strauss is famously level-headed, and he scampered up and down the pitch without allowing the situation to turn into chaos. Weirdly, I started batting well. Before the injury, I'd been batting OK. But now, standing on one leg, the timing was getting sweeter. Perhaps it was because there was no anxiety. Every run was a bonus. Just hit the ball. That was all I could do. Just hit the ball with the middle of the bat. Everything else – the running, the calling, the scampering – was out of my control. Just hit the ball.

Unable to balance properly in the crease while I waited for the ball, I even started to hobble towards the bowler as he was about to bowl. A little forward motion, I guessed, was probably better than standing still and risking falling over again.

After one of these awkward hobbling advances, in which I was about as dynamic as the octogenarian Corporal Jones in *Dad's Army*, I saw the Essex captain Mark Pettini talking animatedly to the umpires. A conference was called in the middle of the pitch. The crowd whistled in impatience. Strauss and I were beckoned to join Pettini and the two umpires.

'Are you really injured?' one of the umpires asked.

Initially, I wasn't sure who he was talking to. It couldn't be me, I assumed. Surely not the person who had collapsed in an undignified heap in front of 20,000? No, surely the question couldn't be addressed to me. It would be too insulting, too stupid.

Pettini confirmed that the question *was* addressed to me. 'I don't mind you having a runner,' he began, 'but you can't start moving your feet like that. Either you're injured or you're not.'

I was dumbstruck. The implication, now I thought about it, was that I was cheating, that I'd faked an ankle injury so that I could get Strauss to run for me because he is a faster runner than me.

In the fifteen years I've known him, that was the only time I ever saw Strauss properly lose his temper. I can't remember what he said, but it ended the argument. Sometimes just seeing someone genuinely outraged has that effect in an argument. Rational words don't always get the message across nearly so effectively as simply showing the emotions that you're feeling. I hope I'd have done the same thing – on his behalf, or any other team-mate's – if the roles had been reversed. It was the instinctive act of a natural team man.

We returned to the game, still shaking our heads, me hobbling and hitting, Strauss calling and running, Morgan making it look easy at the other end. For a while, it was a decent formula. When I'd scored 33, with 20-odd needed to win and plenty of overs left to get them, with the game effectively won, I skied a sweep and was caught. Whatever adrenaline I'd been running on suddenly expired. I wondered if I'd be able to walk off the pitch at all.

Walking off the pitch is usually the loneliest part of the game. You're on your own, as you so often are as a batsman. Alone with your own thoughts, regrets and what-ifs. Alone as you walk off the outfield, alone as you walk up the stairs to the pavilion, even alone – in the true sense of the word – when you rejoin the dressing room. After all, the transition from solitary batsman to social team-player doesn't happen instantly. It takes a while to cast off the carapace. So it is odd walking off with a runner, having a colleague to chat with as the pavilion approaches and the pitch disappears behind you. Thanks, I said. No problem, he replied.

Upstairs, I take my pads off easily but the left boot is stuck. I'm shaking now and my hands aren't moving much better than my feet. The laces are off and I'm tugging at the boot, but it's wedged on, as if it's glued to my foot. I pull it off eventually – it now must be five minutes after I got out – and for the first time I'm scared. The ankle is twice its normal size, as though a tennis ball is growing out from inside the skin. *Elephantiasis of the foot.* It's also starting to turn deep purple, all the way towards the knee, like a chronic case of varicose veins. A bucket arrives, full of water and ice. It's for my foot. I lean over. A part of me wants to be sick into it.

VI

One month later, I was sitting with my girlfriend in a restaurant in central London. My mobile rang, as I was half expecting it to. That day I'd had an MRI scan on my ankle. It was the first time my ankle had been photographed or X-rayed in any way. Why an MRI rather than a normal X-ray? An MRI scan is a sophisticated image designed to highlight any damage to the soft tissues, the ligaments and tendons that are integral to the proper movement of joints.

It was good news, this phone call. It was the doctor who'd sent me to get the MRI scan. There was no serious soft tissue damage, the doctor explained – nothing to worry about on that front.

'Oh great,' I said.

'Yes, exactly,' the doctor said. 'But there was one other little thing.'

'Fire away,' I said, feeling better and better.

'There is a—' There was a slight pause as though quite a simple word was proving a bit of a stumbling block. 'Yes, there's a break in the . . . ankle . . .'

Suddenly, the food didn't taste so good.

The next day, I was staring at an illuminated X-ray of my ankle. I don't know what the inside of an ankle looks like, nor where the bones are supposed to be when they are all intact. So the first thing I said to the doctor, as I searched for the break that I expected to be so small I wouldn't make it out at first, was to seek reassurance. 'Well I assume *that's* not the break,' I said, as I pointed to a broad area of black that was separating two white bones.

It was. There was a displaced fracture of one of the bones in my ankle. Not only was there a clear break, the two broken bones weren't even lined up properly. My left leg was put into a plastic cast – it looks a bit like a moon boot – where it would stay for a long time.

VII

The four weeks between the break at Lord's and the defining evidence of that scan are a blur of meetings and assessments and advice and opinions. I remember the medical team at the club didn't think it was broken. They didn't even take a precautionary X-ray. Before you rush to judge that assessment, I must add that I didn't object to their policy, that I went along with it, even reinforced their sense of optimism. If no one else thought it was broken, I certainly wasn't going to suggest it was.

In fact, one person did think it was broken. My mum had told me the evening it happened. 'I think it's broken,' she said plainly and patiently, as though she knew me well enough to know when I was injured, but also well enough to know I wouldn't listen to her. I didn't.

Instead, I kept saying I'd be fit for the next game. Whatever needed to be done to get me fit, I'd do it.

I was placed on a course of physiotherapy and rehab. One course of treatment was deep tissue massage, thumbs right in, with deep pressure, to 'bring the bruising out'. An associated theory was that the bruising was making my ankle inflexible, which was preventing me from running. So if I could reduce inflexibility and stiffness, I'd be running again in no time – given that no one thought it was broken or anything like that. So I spent long spells stretching the calf muscles as far as I could, 'loosening up the ankle'.

Then there was 'reactivating the muscles' by trying to 'wake them up again'. The way to do this was through bouncing movements. Effectively, I repeatedly hopped up and down on the broken ankle, springing into the air and then landing on it, before springing and landing again – again and again, dozens of times, always on the broken ankle, because that was the one that needed to be 'woken up'. Jumping up and down on a broken ankle, that was the essence of it.

Another activity was a balance-related exercise. I would stand on the broken ankle on a wobble-board for as long as I could before I toppled over. A wobble board is a circular wooden board stuck on the top of a wooden ball about the size of a tennis ball. The idea was to balance on this contraption for as long as I could. Then there was running itself, if you can call it that. I shaved my leg and the ankle would be strapped with sticky tape as tight as possible so I'd be able to 'run' on it.

Throughout all this, I'd be asked to give feedback about how painful it all was. Was it 'manageable'? Yes, I would say, it was manageable. Almost any amount of pain is manageable if you want something enough.

How soon did I start all this rehab? Almost immediately after the injury. I did a full warm-up with the Middlesex team – the running and stretching and fielding practice that takes place before a game – four days after my injury. I didn't play in the game itself. But I hoped that I'd be able to play in *the next game* against my old county, Kent.

'The next game' was a phrase I'd have to get used to. This particular *next game*, when it came, was eight days after the injury. This time I had an actual fitness test before the match – sprinting (or the closest approximation I could manage), changing direction, and so on. But it was no good. I had to admit that I wasn't fit enough to run between the wickets or to field.

Meanwhile, how was the team doing? The winning momentum initially continued. We won the next three games in a row after the game in which I got injured. So that was five consecutive Twenty20 wins, and eight straight wins in all competitions. I've never played in any team, even a school team, that's won *eight* games in a row. We were on fire.

But we lost that game against Kent, and then the next game against Hampshire. We were still top of our Twenty20 group, but we were suddenly not looking so invincible.

The *next game*, I really thought I might play in. It was now twelve days since the injury, and that felt like an awfully long time. And besides, I had a new reason for optimism. I'd become obsessed by ankle braces, as though there was an ankle brace on the market somewhere that would make my injury go away. I took my girlfriend to the John Bell & Croyden physiotherapy shop on Wigmore Street in Marylebone and bought the full set. Ankle straps with plastic splints, ankle straps with elastic, ankle straps with laces, pretty much all the ankle supports they had. My logic was simple: one of them, I reasoned, would be just the right one to make me run smoothly again.

I packed up all the ankle supports with my kit and headed to Uxbridge cricket ground for what might be a decisive qualifying game, again against my old county. As things turned out, none of my braces made the cut, and the physio put his own special strapping on my ankle.

I went out to the practice area, pleased to be in with a chance of playing again. I practised in the batting net to test things out – hitting the ball was fine, and my balance was okay. But when it came to the running part of the fitness test, it just wouldn't get any better. I was still managing only a kind of agonizing mixture of hobbling and jogging. It wouldn't do, I could see that, and again I admitted that I'd failed the fitness test. The good news, as I watched from the sidelines, was that the team returned to winning ways. Six out of eight wins in the Twenty20, and eleven out of thirteen in total.

The hopping, the wobble-boarding, the massaging, the strapping, the practice: I kept up with them all. But as the days slid into weeks, there was a growing realization that the injury couldn't be bounced away, or strapped into insignificance, or even – hardest of all for me to admit – dissolved by an effort of will. I'd never admitted defeat about something I cared about in my life, not once.

We hear a lot about positive thinking, about how if you want something enough you will get it. Well, I have many faults, but a lack of willpower isn't one of them. No amount of willpower, I can see now, could make two broken pieces of bone fuse into a single healthy one.

I was injured, plain and simple, and even though no one yet knew what it was, it was clearly an injury that wasn't getting any better. Some days it felt it was getting worse, and the pain would prevent me from walking, let alone running.

Bad news off the pitch was softened by good news on it. Middlesex were through to the quarter-finals. I, meanwhile, was heading off for that MRI soft-tissue scan, to have special dye injected into my forearm and then have my leg exposed to what looked like a frighteningly evolved washing-machine drum.

That night, over a muted supper, I received that phone call. At last I had to admit that it was serious. I had summoned up every bit of resolve I had to beat an injury I wouldn't fully admit to. But everyone has a breaking point. And I'd reached mine.

I can see now what I couldn't see then. My injury had been a kind of collision between two forces: one was my determination to handle the injury, to master events through a mixture of willpower and medicine, to control my own destiny. The other force was simply bad luck. Bad luck won.

Part II

Questions

5

What is luck?

What do I mean by 'luck'?

Luck is that which is beyond my control. Winning the lottery is luck. My genes are luck. My parents are a matter of luck. It is luck if an opponent drops a catch when I am batting.

But digging deeper into the definition of luck quickly becomes extremely complicated. One of the problems with defining luck is that it belongs to a group of words that are often used interchangeably in conversation but have very distinct meanings.

Consider chance. A mathematician or a card player will tell you that chance is very different from luck. They use chance to mean probability. If you know the chance of an ace being dealt next, you know the probability. In that sense, chance is not at all synonymous with luck. Calculating the chance is a matter of skill; relying on dumb luck is the opposite. You can have 'an even chance' (50 per cent) because chance is calculable. But you can't have 'an even luck'.

In conversational terms, however, the definitions of luck and chance are more overlapping. We say 'It was pure luck that I ran into my friend,' or we could say 'It was pure chance I ran into my friend.' There is not much difference between the two in that human rather than mathematical context. Even here, when they're being used casually, luck and chance aren't identical. Luck implies good luck, whereas chance is more neutral. If you want to say that your luck was bad luck, you have to say so explicitly. 'It was my bad luck to bump into an old friend.'

Luck has this built-in optimism because the English term is derived from the old German word *Gelucke*, which can be translated as both 'luck' and 'happiness'. Some of *Gelucke*'s happiness has survived in the modern English term luck.

If you say, 'I'm feeling lucky today' you don't mean that you expect the day to be determined by chance to an unusual degree. You mean that you think the day will turn out well. 'I'm feeling chancy today,' which does imply that you are ready to take unknown risks, is very different. Jane Austen captured the difference between chance and luck in *Sense and Sensibility* when she wrote: 'The chance proved a lucky one.'

So luck has an optimistic default setting in English. In other languages, it can be the other way around. *Sumphora* in Greek (literally 'carrying together') can mean either 'event' or, more commonly, 'disaster'.

Risk is another slippery word. In the mathematical sense, risk means the probability of a bad event happening, multiplied by the amount of loss if the bad event actually happens. If we bet £100 on the toss of a fair coin (probability 0.5) then the risk is £50 (0.5 multiplied by £100). Probability is the likelihood; risk is the unit of money (or whatever) under threat.

But the connected term 'risky' is commonly used to mean reckless. That dual meaning of risk explains the confusion when we hear complaints about unpopular 'risk-taking bankers'. In one sense it is a tautology. All bankers calculate and act upon assessments of risk: that is what the profession of banking does. In fact, the real and implied complaint against 'risk-taking bankers' is not that they take risks. It's that they take *bad* risks.

This sense that risk implies recklessness is captured in our phrase, 'It's a risk.' Strictly speaking, it is almost meaningless: almost every human action, to some degree, is a risk in the probabilistic sense. There is always a degree of risk when we cross the road, but so long as we do it properly it is not a very large risk. The risk is not risky. So we don't say 'It's a risk' about crossing an *average* road because we reserve the phrase as short-hand for 'It's a big risk'. 'It's a risk' commonly means that the odds are not in our favour.

Randomness is another curveball. Some people casually use randomness to mean odd or idiosyncratic: 'I went to a really random party on Saturday.' But randomness has a very precise mathematical definition. Randomness means it is impossible to use past history to calculate the future probability. For example, a throw of a (fair) die is a random event. If you threw a six last time, you are no more or less likely to throw a six next time. The two throws are independent, random events.

But we often wrongly assume that a random series of coin flips is unlikely to include long, unbroken sequences of heads or tails. It wouldn't be random, would it, if there seemed to be a pattern? But (given a long enough sample) a sequence such as heads–tails–heads–tails–heads–tails is no more random than heads–heads–heads–tails–tails–tails. We tend (wrongly) to associate randomness with constant flux.

When Apple introduced its Shuffle player that mixes up songs at random, listeners complained that the same sequences of songs kept recurring. So Apple modified Shuffle to make it *seem* more random by artificially ruling out patterns that in fact used to occur purely by chance. As Steve Jobs put it, 'We're making the Shuffle less random to make it feel more random.' Weird but true – and a testament to how people misunderstand randomness. Randomness doesn't mean constant change; it means perfect unpredictability.

Understanding randomness helps you to understand that some games require an entirely unpredictable strategy. Most people know the game Rock–Paper–Scissors (sometimes called Spoof). Each player must simultaneously make a gesture with his hand that signifies either rock (clenched fist), or paper (flat palm) or scissors (index and third finger parted). Paper beats rock, rock beats scissors, scissors beats paper. So each move is equally likely, in principle, to win a single contest. It all depends on what the other players do.

We sometimes played Rock–Paper–Scissors in the dressing room when I was a cricketer. For example, two captains might play the game to decide which team would bat first in a practice match. Despite being useless at most dressing-room pastimes, I was surprisingly good at Rock–Paper–Scissors. Why? Because the optimal strategy is a perfectly random one. As neither paper, scissors nor rock is inherently superior to the other two, you cannot be a good player, only a bad one. Bad players have a plan, a series of moves arranged in advance. 'Good' players decide at random. I had the advantage of knowing that playing dumb was as clever as you could be.

My opponents would say, 'I know what Ed is thinking, he's is going to triple bluff me with a rock because he went scissors last time.' No, I really wasn't. I just made it up on the spot. You cannot gain an advantage with a strategy, you can only hand your opponent an advantage by giving him clues about what you're thinking. The only 'skill' in spoof is the ability to think randomly rather than in patterns.

Serendipity is another word in the luck family. Invented by Horace Walpole in 1754, it appropriately began life as a misprint. Walpole wrote a letter to Horace Mann developing the idea of serendipity from a 'silly fairytale' about chance called *The Three Princes of Serendip*. But Walpole had made a mistake: the real title of the story was *The Three Princes of Sarendip* (the ancient name for Sri Lanka).

Before its current fashionable renaissance, serendipity had almost disappeared from popular usage. The LexisNexis database of newspapers and magazines reveal two appearances for serendipity in the whole of the 1960s. In the 1990s its usages jumped to 13,266. When a poll of favourite words was recently conducted at the London Festival of Literature, serendipity headed the list, beating even Jesus and money (joint equal in tenth place).

Serendipity's meaning has been watered down with its popularity. Its real definition is finding something that you are *explicitly not looking for*. So it is *not* serendipity to meet your girlfriend at a singles' bar: that's why you went there in the first place. But it *is* serendipity if you meet your future wife on a train neither of you meant to catch, at a time when romantic entanglement could not have been further from your mind. More on this later.

The bigger picture is no less opaque. The foundation of this whole series of concepts is fortune, and the Roman goddess Fortuna (and her Greek cousin Tyche). But fortune was actually a force before she became a goddess. The Greeks and the early Romans wrote about Fortuna as a terrifying, unknowable power, greater even than the gods. Only later, as the cult of Fortuna grew, was fortune increasingly personified as a goddess. In classical terms, fortune – what we now call luck – initially trumped deity, not vice versa.

Fortune was closely tied to another central classical idea: fate. In one sense, fate is like the modern concept of luck in that it is entirely beyond your control. And yet, in another sense, fate is the opposite of luck. Fate is set in stone. Modern luck is not: it is unfixed, capricious and unpredictable.

Shall we recap? Chance can mean the same as luck or something very different; risk can mean both probabilistic loss and also recklessness; luck is derived from and also opposite to the classical idea of fate; and fortune was a force as well as a goddess.

That's that sorted, then. In fact, given the slipperiness of the word, I'll just stick with what I started with. *Luck is what happens to me that is outside my control.*

6

Not making your own luck

I

When you are writing a book about luck, you are bombarded by people who ask if your book is about 'making our own luck'. I have two replies, one short, the other long. The first is 'No', the second is book-length. Perhaps I should be more helpful. If you are seeking the particular chapter on 'making your own luck', or not making your own luck, this is it.

I was having lunch in a restaurant sitting opposite one of the most enviable men I've met. Annoyingly handsome, athletic, highly intelligent, he is also possessed of the kind of innate self-assurance that seems only to belong to a certain type of American man. He has just married one of my university friends, Hermione, and it doesn't take long to figure out what she saw in this Andrew guy.

We're having lunch across the street from his home in a discreet corner of London's Bayswater, a quiet, civilized road that leads to Hyde Park. In fact, he ran past me in the park yesterday, running fast and making it look easy, hungrily eating up the ground as though it posed an insufficient challenge.

We're meeting because our last conversation was dominated by the subject of luck – his good luck. Not everyone would see it that way, but that's how Andrew interpreted it. In one sense, that's not unusual: most people have a story about luck. They just aren't as interesting as Andrew's.

He reminds me how it starts. 'It was about 11.30 at night. We'd all had a few tequilas at a Mexican-themed dinner party in north London. From what I understand, I was in the middle of laughing when suddenly I stopped, lurched forward and banged my head on the table, reared up, turned towards Hermione and collapsed into her arms. The other guests dragged me to the sofa. That's it. I don't remember anything from about 6 p.m. that day until six days later.'

He'd had a massive cardiac arrest.

To say Andrew is not cardiac-arrest material would be a serious understatement. I reckon I'm fairly fit. In comparison with him, I'm a lazy slob. He doesn't go for jogs. He goes running up hills in the pouring rain, pushing himself to the limits of his aerobic capacity. That may well have been one of the only things within his control that helped to save his life.

He is disarmingly prepared to piece together the details of the evening. 'Very fortunately – that's what I would say, fortunately – the guy whose house it was had just come back from two years in Afghanistan. He was an aid worker, so he was well trained in CPR [cardiopulmonary resuscitation]. Lucas jumped on top of me and instantly started pumping my heart. I was also lucky it hadn't happened six months earlier when we'd been living in Rwanda – not top of the tables for emergency medical services.'

Unprompted, Andrew lists the other ways in which he was 'lucky' that night. 'I was even luckier that I was at that house at all when it happened. I work from home so 95 per cent of my day is either by myself or with people who wouldn't have known what to do. So it was quite extraordinary that Lucas was there. In almost any other situation . . .'

He trails off, not sadly, but as though words aren't needed to express how probable it is he would have died if his cardiac arrest had happened during the 95 per cent of his life when he wasn't around people trained in CPR. 'Friends at the party went out on the street to look out for the ambulance. A policeman just happened to be walking by. He came up to the flat and he and Lucas rotated doing CPR while they waited for the ambulance.'

As Andrew goes through the story, I am looking for signs of distress, but I can't see any. 'For forty-five minutes I was flat-lining with occasional stutterings to life. I don't think it was *complete* flat-lining, because that means . . . because that means you don't have much going on. Occasionally there would be a bit of life and I would take gasps for breath. Then it would stop again and there'd be nothing. At the flat, the ambulance crew tried to restart my heart four times using a defibrillator. They finally stabilized me enough to try to get me to hospital. They put me in a sheet and they dragged me down the narrow staircase.'

The scene must have put incredible strain on those who were with him. 'They made Hermione go upstairs into another room while they were pumping. Sitting up in that room, what do you say? To whom do you turn? If you're not religious, and can't pray to God, what do you do? What do the gamblers say when they're in Vegas and hoping they will win against all the odds?' He laughs at the thought, knowing how easy it is for even the most dedicated sceptic to turn to God when they are really desperate. '"Go science!" isn't that snappy, is it?'

No, it isn't. Many more, surely, follow the pattern described in the famous Arthur Hugh Clough poem 'There is No God':

And almost everyone when age,
Disease, or sorrows strike him,
Inclines to think there is a God,
Or something very like Him.

Which of us, as your fiancé receives CPR while you are kept in a distant corner of the hospital, would stay true to their atheistic 'beliefs'? How tempting it must have been to make one little prayer, just one, to someone, to anyone. I sense that Andrew is very proud of the fact that such a prayer was never made, that Hermione didn't turn to God. It was 'Go science!' all the way.

Andrew, the doctors eventually discovered, has arrhythmogenic right ventricular cardiomyopathy, or ARVC. It is a genetic disease caused by defects within parts of the heart muscle. Effectively, the walls of your heart deteriorate to the point of collapse. 'About one in 10,000 people have it. But most people die on the pitch, as it were.' The sporting metaphor is Andrew's, not mine. 'You hear about the American footballer who collapses on the pitch and dies even though he's really fit. It's odd that a professional sportsman, surrounded by medical people, wouldn't survive. But even *they* don't always make it.'

Having not died on the pitch, Andrew found himself at University College Hospital in London, one of the few hospitals in Britain that are pioneering a new technique to treat cardiac arrests by cooling the body by 3–4°C to reduce the stress on the brain and vital organs. But the prognosis was bleak, even if he lived: 'The suggestion was that even if I made it, I was going to have brain damage. My kidneys failed and they almost had to take out a huge chunk of the intestines because they thought they were ruined. But gradually I improved.'

Eventually they stopped sedation and slowly brought him out of a coma. 'The first thing I remember was the next Thursday, six days after the fateful dinner. I remember waking up and hearing Hermione say: "You had a cardiac arrest and your mother's here." I remember immediately thinking, "My *mother's* here?"' (She lives in Seattle.)

Not only was he conscious, it quickly became clear that Andrew's brain was entirely undamaged. It was, in medical terms, very close to inexplicable.

The odds do not bear thinking about. Had he been alone; had Lucas not been well trained in CPR; had the policeman not randomly walked past the house; had the advice from 999 been less well judged; had he not collapsed near to one of the world's leading hospitals for this kind of problem. Had any one of those circumstances been different, Andrew would either have died or have suffered huge brain damage. Instead, he is eating *linguine vongole* in a London restaurant, looking brilliantly healthy, still running in the park and planning a skiing trip to the Alps.

It is no surprise that common speech morphs into religious language. *Saved.* There is a powerful human instinct to assume that there must have been more to it than sheer luck.

'A lot of people said, "It's going to change your life, it's going to make you more religious. Are you going to church?"' He pauses, with a wry expression, as though he doesn't want to be too dogmatic. 'My response was, "Interesting you should say that, but that wasn't my reaction."' The wry expression turns into something more openly amused. 'At the back of my mind, I'm thinking, "And all these kids who die from ARVC – are we supposed to think God doesn't love them?" I think it's pretty egotistical to think that I'm the one who gets chosen to stay alive.'

Ironically, Andrew was once a firm believer in a providential God. 'When a client told me, "God must have a special plan for you," I replied, "Had you said that to me ten years ago, I probably would have believed you." But now I can't see the logic of that. Think about it. If something good happens, people assume it's divine intervention. But when something bad happens, they don't.'

It's true. Venice was devastated by the plague in 1630. When the pandemic eventually subsided, the Republic vowed to build and dedicate a church as a votive offering for the city's deliverance. The result was Baldassare Longhena's Basilica di Santa Maria della Salute. 'Salute' means simply deliverance. It seemed appropriate to thank God for stopping the plague, but not to blame him for sending it.

Clearly, his cardiac arrest has been a test of Andrew's faith: his faith in atheism. 'Previously I would have seen it through a religious perspective. That God wanted me to be at that house for dinner that night. He wanted those people to be there. He used those people.' Andrew is smiling at the easiness of it all. 'Everything is very explicable with that philosophy. Your relationship with that power makes you feel good. A lot of my family and friends in the US will think that. They'll hope that someday I'll see the light and I'll come back to Jesus because of this.'

If Andrew still resists faith, how about the concept of fate? Does he feel that there is some way in which the cardiac arrest was designed to send him on a new path, to discover a sense of calling?

'No. I guess I just think my number wasn't up. There's a law of large numbers. How many people get this: one in

10,000. I was just one of the people that happened not to die from this. A case of failed "sudden-death syndrome".'

In some ways, it's the hardest explanation of all: that there is no explanation.

III

But that doesn't mean that Andrew is entirely unchanged. 'In America, this would have cost me £200,000. But in Britain everyone takes a little bit of a financial hit for me and, hopefully, society is better for it.' A nationalized health service is a way of pooling risks to protect those who are unlucky, a compulsory insurance policy operated by the state. When you are the person who needs help, when your survival depends on the pooling of risks and the sharing of resources, you see that more clearly.

Perhaps that is why his cardiac arrest reinforced Andrew's liberalism. He could easily have travelled in the opposite political direction. 'As an entrepreneur, being someone who is trying to generate my own wealth, I was more likely to move to the right, maybe take my business away from Britain. Now, I'll stay here and pay back some of those taxes!' Don't worry, I reassure him, the borders are closed until we've got our £200,000 back.

'Unquestionably I was lucky. But what does luck mean? Some things that used to be explained as luck we now fully understand through science. For now, we can't explain why

I survived and why I still have my brain functioning. But one day they will explain it. So it will no longer be a question of luck. It'll just be science.'

What Andrew means is that in one sense luck is only a useful concept when we don't know the real causes. We've hit upon a recurrent disagreement about the definition of luck. 'Had somebody done CPR badly and I'd died,' Andrew asks, 'would that have been bad luck or could it have been easily scientifically explained as ineptitude?'

I reply that it would have been a matter of ineptitude to the medic, but still bad luck for the victim. You're unlucky if you're exposed to ineptitude at a critical moment in your life. Luck need not be a mystery. An event can be clearly 'caused' and yet also be luck: it depends on your perspective.

In more practical terms, Andrew's cardiac arrest has reinforced his conviction that it is absurd to think we always 'make our own luck'. 'It's always the successful people who say that. There's a self-selection bias. People who have had bad luck don't get a voice. No one listens to someone who says, "I had terrible luck" because nobody wants to listen to losers.'

Having been exposed to real luck, Andrew has reconsidered the concept of success in business. 'Yes, I feel that I can put myself in as good a position as possible in business. On the upside, I might happen to be in the right place at the right time and do well. But on the downside, things like what happened to my health can happen to anyone's business. You can't control that. And people who say that they can control those things, that you always make your own luck ...'

It's as though there isn't a word even in Andrew's vocabulary to express the appropriate degree of disdain. 'Well, they can believe that if they want to.'

The waiter arrives offering coffee. I wonder if a double espresso is sensible? 'Coming from Seattle,' he says, 'life without coffee wouldn't be worth it.' I also remind Andrew that I saw him sprinting past me in the park yesterday. Perhaps Hermione should follow him with a speed gun, making sure he isn't running too fast and raising his heart rate to dangerous levels.

We laugh. Surely it's best, after all this, not to push your luck *too* far?

7

Anti-luck

I

It sounds strange to write that the concept of luck is always under attack. But it is. It's inevitable, if you think about it. Admitting the existence of luck demands the acknowledgement that some things are beyond our control, and the control-freak side of human nature is never going to accept such an uncomfortable state of affairs without a fight.

The Victorians, unsurprisingly, took up the battle with particular enthusiasm. Eighteen-fifty-nine was a good year for publishing. It was the year that both Darwin's *On The Origin of Species* and John Stuart Mill's *On Liberty* came into print. But another book published in 1859 outsold both Mill and Darwin. It was Samuel Smiles's *Self-Help*, a bestseller that helped to shape what became known as Victorian values. The book's first line, 'Heaven helps those who help themselves', encapsulated the sense that success was within everyone's grasp. It was an unashamed primer in getting on.

Self-Help was a smash success, selling 20,000 copies in its first year. In fact, only the Bible outsold *Self-Help* over the next hundred years, and many Victorians kept the two books next to each other. When Smiles died, his funeral cortège was second in size only to Queen Victoria's.

It will not surprise you to learn that, as the father of self-help, Smiles didn't think much of luck. It was simply self-pity:

> Misfortune is next door to Stupidity; and it will often be found that men are constantly lamenting their luck, are in some way or other reaping the consequences of their own neglect, mismanagement, improvidence, or want of application. Dr. Johnson ... has honestly said: 'All the complaints which are made of the world are unjust; I never knew a man of merit neglected; it was generally by his own fault that he failed of success.'

The world according to *Self-Help* is determined by hard work and industry. Luck is an irrelevance: 'Steady attention to detail lies at the root of human progress, and diligence, above all, is the mother of good luck ... Accident does very little towards the production of any great result in life.'

We can only guess what Smiles would have made of the subsequent chance inventions in medicine and business. In 1928, Alexander Fleming picked up a culture plate of the Staphylococcus bacteria that he had left on a bench. A contaminating mould had grown on the dish, which had

killed off nearby bacterial colonies. This 'mould juice' became
the basis of penicillin, one of the greatest life-savers in human
history. It was not all luck, of course. It was *not* luck that
Fleming noticed the mould had formed. But it was luck that he
had accidentally created the right conditions in the first place
– a nice example of Pasteur's dictum that 'Chance favours the
prepared mind.'

Luck has also provided businesses with their critical opportunities. In fact, you may well be sitting near one of the most
popular pieces of office equipment ever invented: the Post-it
note. The US manufacturer 3M had invented a glue that
didn't work very well; for six years, it was left on the shelf
unused. Then an employee discovered that this bad glue
could remedy a problem he had with flapping hymn-book
pages. But it was only when Post-its were given to their
secretaries that 3M realized they had discovered a phenomenon – by mistake.

Smiles's narrative style, in contrast, was to pile on example
after example of success stories that, in his opinion, had
nothing to do with luck:

> Nor have the most distinguished artists of our own country
> been born in a position more than ordinarily favourable to
> the culture of artistic genius. Gainsborough and Bacon were
> the sons of cloth-workers ... Lawrence was the son of a
> publican, and Turner of a barber ... It was not by luck or
> accident that these men achieved distinction, but by sheer
> industry and hard work.

Smiles even had a neat put-down for the concept of genius:

'It is patience.'

With its celebration of grit and graft and rags-to-riches success stories you might expect *Self-Help* to have been written by an American rather than a Scot. In fact, some passages sound very close to the American Dream adapted for the British. You do not need God-given talent. You do not need opportunity or fortune. In *Self-Help*, you simply require the typically Victorian values of dedication, fortitude, hard work and perseverance. By trying to prove that its readers did not need luck, *Self-Help* promised them that success was within their own grasp.

Self-Help was one of Lady Thatcher's favourite books. She, too, didn't think much of luck. As a ten-year-old, she won her school's recital prize. 'You were lucky, Margaret,' her teacher told her. 'I wasn't lucky, I deserved it,' Margaret replied. Maybe she was right on that occasion. And we shouldn't read too much into a childhood story. But the less attractive face of Thatcherism was the perception that failure was always the fault of those who failed.

The same objection can be levelled at *Self-Help*. Though much of it is unobjectionable common sense, it is only a short jump from the implications of *Self-Help* to a more sinister philosophy. What about people who don't succeed? If success is caused by effort alone, surely those who fail deserve to fail? Smiles tried to square this circle by claiming in his preface not to be interested in outcomes, only in intentions. It's the effort that counts. Smiles approvingly quotes from Joseph Addison's play *Cato*:

> 'Tis not in mortals to command success;
> We'll do more, Sempronius, we'll deserve it.

But *Self-Help* was not read in the spirit of Addison's noble sentiment. It heralded a harsher, more modern tone. You could, indeed you must, pull yourself up by your bootstraps. Read on, it said, and you'll learn how. Millions did read on. *Self-Help* wasn't just a bestseller. It was the beginning of a genre: *Self-Help* the book begat self-help the industry.

II

A century and a half later, the industry has never been more profitable. In 2009 Amazon sold 45,000 different titles in its self-help section, making self-help worth £10 billion annually. Inevitably, the relationship between self-help and luck has evolved. Smiles argued that luck didn't exist. It is now more fashionable to argue that luck can be entirely *controlled*. Luck is out there, waiting to be grabbed with both hands, and several of the most wildly successful books in recent years have promised to give their readers the gift of eternal good fortune. Arguing that luck doesn't exist and arguing that you can control it are, of course, two ways of saying the same thing – but we'll come to that in a second.

The most famous example of this 'Be lucky!' self-help industry is Rhonda Byrne's *The Secret*. For the price of a £12 hardback, you never have to worry about bad luck again. *Self-Help* argued you didn't need advantages, just perseverance. *The Secret*, as befits its hazier New Age sensibilities, says you just have to *believe*.

The Secret promises that having faith in 'the law of attraction' will always give you what you want. The idea is pretty simple. If you focus on what you want, and believe you will get it, then hey presto, you do. Want to be thin? Think thin and you will be. Want to be rich? Think rich and you will be. Want to park your car? Think parking space and one will open up. If you're falling out of an aircraft, think ... Oops, that didn't work. The law of gravity trumps the law of attraction, as one American comedian put it.

External circumstances or opportunities do not exist in *The Secret*. The answers to all your problems reside within your own beliefs. Here is Ms Byrne's explanation of natural or man-made disasters:

> In a large-scale tragedy, like 9/11, Hurricane Katrina, etc., we see that the law of attraction responds to people being at the wrong place at the wrong time because their dominant thoughts were on the same frequency of such events ... If their dominant thoughts and feelings were in alignment with the energy of fear, separation, powerlessness and having no

control over outside circumstances, then that is what they attracted.

Remember, while many people died in these tragic events, there were also many miraculous stories of survival, and the same can be said about those people whose thoughts were in alignment with the energy of unity, love, oneness and joy with the universe.

This comes dangerously close to implying that it's your fault if you find yourself in the middle of a hurricane, or, indeed, a holocaust. So think carefully the next time you tell someone that we all 'make our own luck'. First, it is an oxymoron. Luck is something beyond your control. If you make your own luck, it is clearly not luck you are making. The second problem is much more serious. If we do all make our own luck, it is a clear sentence of guilt on everyone who encounters misfortune.

In the DVD of *The Secret*, a woman claims to have cured herself of breast cancer in three months. A friend of mine recently died of breast cancer. It would be hard to imagine a braver, more forthright foe to undertake a 'battle against cancer'. But the cancer won, eventually, as cancers often do. That her death could be interpreted as a failure of willpower or positive thinking or whatever mumbo-jumbo the self-help snake-oil salesmen have cooked up is a gross insult. As her husband perfectly put it: 'The last thing we need is more of that Lance Armstrong "It's your fault if you don't cure yourself of cancer" bullshit.'

III

In *The Pleasures and Sorrows of Work*, the philosopher Alain de Botton argues that the self-help version of history – you can be whatever you want to be – was unknown to the ancients and is a distinctive feature of modern society. De Botton's intelligent and provocative book has nothing whatever to do with the dishonest banalities of *The Secret*. But he does argue that the idea of 'making your own luck' fits our world:

> In older, more hierarchical societies, an individual's fate had largely been decided by the accidents of birth ... However, in the meritocratic, socially mobile modern world, one's status might now well be determined by one's confidence, imagination and ability to convince others of one's due.
>
> ... The weight accorded to ideas of nurture and to the development of self-esteem in theories of modern education no longer seemed like a sign that our societies had gone mad or soft. On the contrary, this emphasis was as finely attuned to the demands of contemporary working life as instruction in stoicism and physical bravery had been to the exigencies of ancient times. It owed its existence less to kindness than to practical necessity. Like the rearing methods of every age, it was intended to ensure that the young would be granted the optimal chances of survival in a hostile environment.

De Botton's logic suggests that we can no longer bear to believe in luck. We cannot afford to. Luck might have suited the 'exigencies of ancient times', when Stoics found solace in dignity if they were confronted by forces beyond their control. But we have moved on from a world determined by fate and luck. 'Our meritocratic, socially mobile modern world', he argues, has no need for the idea of luck. We have progressed far beyond the unfair predestination of privilege. Success is now determined by talent plus hard work. We ought to believe that we completely control our own destinies, but is it true?

America, for instance, prides itself on 'the American Dream', in which there is no barrier or impediment to talent and hard work. But a 2010 study by the Organization for Economic Co-operation and Development found that social mobility in the US was lower than in Australia, Canada and the Nordic countries. The Economic Mobility Project made similar findings, showing that parental income is a better predictor of a child's future in America than in many countries in Europe. It seems the poor in America – the land of the free – are much less likely to improve their status than American rhetoric would have us believe. In Britain, too, social mobility seems to have stalled, or even gone into reverse.

It is obviously true that modern Western societies are less determined by privilege than the hierarchical society of imperial Rome. But that does not mean that our age is as mobile and meritocratic as we believe it to be.

What is interesting is the discrepancy between myth and reality. The language of self-determination has increased – social mobility, self-help, making your own luck. But that aspiration is not reflected in reality. We may be buying more books than ever to learn how to 'make our own luck', but it doesn't seem to be working. So we are obstructed, in language and in thought, from bridging the gap between the mantras of self-help and the realities of life. We remain a *fortunocracy* confused by the rhetoric of a meritocracy.

A most uncomfortable question follows. Must there not be a point at which the philosophy of self-help and positive thinking borders on cruelty? Might it not be the case that believing in 'making your own luck' is serving only to make us unhappy and confused?

IV

The fight against luck extends far beyond self-help. Religion, too, has often been at war with luck.

If you Google the words luck and Christianity, you will be bombarded by angry American pastors – Texas seems to be a particular hot-bed of luck-hating pastors – telling you that luck is one of the most evil myths ever invented. Luck is blasphemy, nothing less. It suggests the existence of a rival Higher Power. In their opinion, there is only God.

Luck denial isn't restricted to the far-out evangelicals. At a party, I told an Anglican priest that I was writing a book about luck. 'No such thing!' he shot back. Admitting the existence of luck was an affront to Divine Providence. I was, I must admit, a little surprised to hear that such views were still current. I knew vaguely about the Christian philosopher Boethius, whose Wheel of Fortune revised man's relationship with fate. Gone, in Boethius's world picture, was the classical concept of Fortuna, the beautiful goddess whom you could influence or even befriend.

Boethius recast Fortuna – now an agent of a Christian God – as a blind old hag who was coldly indifferent to human suffering. The Wheel of Fortune turned inexorably. Everything was fixed by providential fate. It seemed rude, at the time, to remind the priest that Boethius was writing in *the sixth century*. And if everything can really be explained as part of God's will, as the priest's logic implied, does that include pandemics, plagues, famines, floods and human catastrophes?

V

Then there are the rocket scientists of finance. They don't like luck, either. When I started writing this book, Mike Atherton, the former England cricket captain, and now journalist and author, lent me a well-thumbed paperback of Peter L. Bernstein's *Against the Gods: The Remarkable Story of Risk*. Bernstein's book, first published in 1996, is possibly the best book ever written about luck. But luck is the book's anti-hero rather than its hero. Bernstein argues that the relevance of luck is in retreat, that it has been gradually supplanted by a more scientific understanding of the world. Luck is portrayed as a gloomy and unhelpful fog, slowly being burned away by the light of human progress.

That progress, Bernstein argues, is embodied by the concept of risk:

> The revolutionary idea that defines the boundary between modern times and the past is the mastery of risk: the notion that the future is more than a whim of the gods and that men are not passive before nature. Until human beings discovered a way across that boundary, the future was ... the murky domain of oracles and soothsayers who held a monopoly over knowledge of future events.

The useful concept of risk, according to Bernstein, had helped to free society from the shackles of fate and superstition. Bernstein's heroes range from Renaissance gamblers to the inventors of modern financial models. Their urge to predict, to calculate and to quantify had beaten back the forces of rogue chance.

It was unfortunate that Bernstein, who was such a firm believer that modern finance was marching towards Apollonian clarity and order, should have died in 2009, when financial theory was at such a low ebb. He made the case for financial progress and optimism with clarity and intellectual generosity. But some of the ideas in *Against the Gods*, exploited by less modest and intellectually curious minds than

Bernstein's, resurfaced on the wrong side of history during the 2007–9 financial crisis.

Where Bernstein imagined a world in which mastery of risk had supplanted the backward idea of luck, others claimed to have achieved this state of utopia. The classic case study of financiers claiming to have defeated luck was the now notorious Black-Scholes formula. This formula, devised in 1973 by Myron Scholes and Fischer Black, automatically priced derivative 'options'. It won Scholes the 1997 Nobel Prize and became widely used throughout the financial sector.

According to the Black-Scholes formula, successful investment no longer required 'gut instincts', or 'good judgement' – or even good fortune. Instead, they had invented a method of making money without any chance of losing. 'In a strict sense, there wasn't any risk,' Professor Merton Miller put it, '*if* [my italics] the world behaved as it did in the past.' Black-Scholes had apparently turned making money into a science that couldn't go wrong.

Nirvana, it seemed, had arrived. Trading was no longer subject to chance at all: it was pure science. Myron Scholes was confident that the theory would make him not only a celebrated academic but also exceptionally rich. Alongside fellow Nobel Laureate Robert C. Merton, in 1995 Scholes founded the hedge fund Long Term Capital Management.

The story of LTCM was superbly chronicled by Roger Lowenstein in his book *When Genius Failed*. In its precision and assumptions, LTCM mimicked the physical sciences. One line in the Black-Scholes formula points out that it relies upon 'ideal conditions'. Prices were assumed to behave like molecules in a bell-jar. The behaviour of any one molecule might be random, but taken as a group the molecules would distribute themselves in a perfectly predictable fashion.

Black–Scholes implied that old-fashioned investors, people who played the stock market according to judgements or gut instinct, were involved in ascientific games of pure chance. Remember the murky world of 'oracles and soothsayers'? Investors of this kind didn't warrant much serious analysis. If enough people are engaged in coin flipping, someone has to win. That didn't mean the winning coin-flipper had the ability to make the coin come up heads. It was just the luck of the toss. LTCM, on the other hand, believed it had literally found the formula for making money. Uncertainty had been banished. They weren't gamblers; they were scientists. 'We're not just building a fund,' Scholes explained, 'we're a financial technology company.'

How did their fund do in the real world? In LTCM's first year they rewarded investors with 20 per cent profit, followed by 43 per cent in the second year and 41 per cent in the third. Nirvana seemed to be working.

But LTCM couldn't cope when the financial environment no longer matched the assumptions used in their formula. First, Asia suffered a financial crisis in 1997, then the Russian government defaulted on its loans in 1998. Scholes watched in horror as his formula stopped working: 'After the Russian default, the relations [in his model] that tended to exist in the recent past seemed to disappear.'

In other words prices were no longer moving like random particles in a bell-jar. They were moving all in alignment: towards panic. It was a possibility that LTCM had left out of their equations.

LTCM's models told them they shouldn't expect to lose more than $50 million on any given day, *ever*. But four days after Russia defaulted, they dropped half a *billion* dollars in one day. The concept of finance without chance or uncertainty had gone spectacularly bust.

Reflecting on the collapse of LTCM, Merton Miller conveniently wondered whether 'the disaster was merely a unique and isolated event, a bad drawing from nature's urn?' In fact, the problem wasn't 'a bad drawing from nature's urn'. It was the idea that there *couldn't be* a bad drawing from nature's urn. The problem wasn't bad luck. It was the vainglorious refusal to believe in bad luck.

LTCM proved a prophetic dry-run for the full-blown financial crisis a decade later. This time, the problems did not begin in a single private hedge fund. They revolved around international investment banks, which also used Black-Scholes-type mathematical models.

'Events that models only predicted would happen once in 10,000 years happened every day for three days.' That was the conclusion of Matthew Rothman, a quantitative risk expert at Lehman Brothers when it collapsed. Even ten years after the warning shot fired by the collapse of LTCM, the 'scientists' of risk were incredulous once again.

In the financial crisis of 2007–9, of course, the taxpayer

ended up picking up the bill (unlike the collapse of LTCM, which was bailed out by private money). The underlying paradox is unavoidable. The dizzying ascent of the science of risk – and the corresponding banishment of any role for chance or uncertainty – culminated in a sharp descent of the taxpayers' money.

No wonder there is an old joke about economics: it's the only would-be science in which if the world isn't like the model, then it's the world's problem.

The financial wizards extended their contempt for luck to life in general. Consider this interview from 2008, given by Professor Robert E. Lucas, Nobel Laureate in Economics:

Q: Do you feel that capitalism generates a long-run equilibrium distribution that we can live with?

A: Absolutely ... Now is there too much inequality? I don't see it. I think people who drop out of high school, take drugs and so on are going to be poorer than the guys who worked hard. It doesn't bother me at all. Why shouldn't they be poor? It's hard to work!

Q: You think the distribution of income reflects effort more than it does, say, luck?

A: Both. But how do you get all this luck? How did Bill Gates get all this good luck? He wasn't sitting on his ass smoking dope or something like that!

William James Earle, Professor of Philosophy at Baruch College in New York, came up with the perfect riposte to

Lucas's bleak logic that success and failure are always deserved. 'Forty-four million Americans lived in poverty in 2009: taking Lucas's explanation of poverty seriously for the moment raises the question of whether there really was that much dope to go around.'

VI

It is quite a broad church, then, this anti-luck constituency. It numbers among its congregation an extraordinary range of people and professions – Victorian self-help authors, New Age positive thinkers, religious literalists, derivatives traders. Each, in their wildly different ways, has an alternative theory in place of luck – hard work, or faith, or God, or probability theory. There are, it would seem, greater numbers on their side of the argument than mine.

But possibly the most celebrated anti-luck slogan comes from the world of sport. 'That was lucky,' a journalist said to the golf champion Gary Player after he holed an iron shot to win a tournament. Player's reply has become the most quoted line in the history of sport: 'The more I practise, the luckier I get.' What began as a put-down to a hapless reporter has hardened into conventional wisdom. You 'earn' luck through practice, or so it is drummed into every young sportsman.

We know, of course, that Player's dictum is another version of the ideal of 'making your own luck'. It belongs to the long-standing tradition of trying to convert luck into something you can control. Yet as a competitive strategy there is clearly some truth in Player's one-liner. A sportsman who hones his skills and technique gives himself the best chance of playing good shots and winning championships.

Nonetheless, we should examine whether the unfortunate journalist immortally slapped down by Player was in fact correct. Do you need luck to hit an iron shot straight into the hole? I put that question to the man who knows more about holes-in-one than anyone in the history of European golf: Colin Montgomerie. Only three players have won more tournaments than Montgomerie in the history of the European Tour. And no one has hit more holes-in-one: Montgomerie's ninth hole-in-one took him past Bernhard Langer's eight.

Standing on the driving range of the magnificent Scottish course Gleneagles, I spoke to Montgomerie about luck and skill, and how people often confuse the two. Gleneagles is home territory for Montgomerie. He was educated at Strathallan School (he is another top British sportsman who benefited from private schooling), which is a few miles from the 1920s grandeur of Gleneagles. As a boy, he played golf at Glen Devon, just along the valley that runs through the Ochil Hills. With Scottish rain lashing at our golf clubs, I asked him whether you needed some luck to make a hole-in-one. 'That's a very good question,' he replied, smiling as though it was an uncomfortable niggle that he had long considered but always avoided directly confronting.

Glancing back towards the first tee, where the Ryder Cup

will begin in 2014, Montgomerie began to laugh at the absurdity of golfing logic. 'To hit a ball 1.68 inches wide for 200 yards straight into a cup 4.25 inches wide? Yes, you definitely need luck to do that. Think about what happens to the ball during a hole-in-one. It flies through the wind. It bounces on the ground. It rolls along the turf. You cannot entirely control the bounce of the ball or the journey of the ball on the grass. Let's be honest. To put the ball close to the hole is skill; to put the ball *in* the hole needs luck.'

Montgomerie added that the connoisseur's shot is not the hole-in-one. It is the almost-hole-in-one. 'In fact, a hole-in-one isn't the best shot you can play. What you're really trying to do is to leave it "stiff" [that means leaving the ball one foot or so from the hole].' Pro golfers direct their approach shots according to the topography of the green. They like to leave the ball just below the hole, owing to the fact that uphill putts are regarded as easier and less risky than downhill ones.

If the ball happens actually to roll *into* the hole, it was probably slightly mishit by the golfer – it hadn't quite slowed down enough when it reached the hole. So a hole-in-one not only requires the co-operation of inanimate forces and objects such as the grass and the wind. It also relies on the minuscule *under*performance of the golfer himself. 'In fact, of my nine holes-in-one, only two were what I would call perfect shots. The other seven relied on the roll of the ball.' In other words, seven out of Montgomerie's nine hole-in-ones were slight mishits!

So I asked him how many really perfect shots – shots that feel unimprovable when the club makes contact with the ball

– he hits in a typical day. 'You hit maybe only three or four perfect shots in a round of seventy-two shots.'

That is about one in twenty perfect strikes of the golf ball. It might not sound like a lot. But consider how many shots Montgomerie has hit during his twenty-five-year career: hundreds of tournaments, thousands of rounds, hundred of thousands of shots – one in twenty of which felt absolutely perfect. And yet all those perfect shots have resulted in only nine holes-in-one – and that's more than anyone in the history of European golf. The rest, the forgotten thousands of perfect strikes, finished up falling short of a perfect outcome.

Let's recap. The aim of golf is to get the ball into the hole in as few shots as possible. And yet most holes-in-one aren't perfect shots. And the vast majority of perfect shots don't end up as holes-in-one. The optimal shot (leaving it stiff) has a sub-optimal outcome, and a sub-optimal shot has an optimal outcome (the hole-in-one). No wonder Montgomerie smiled when I asked the question. It is enough to send you mad.

There is, we have discovered, a clear difference between making perfect contact with the golf ball (which is in your control) and getting a perfect outcome (which is partly beyond your control). And yet every golfer, on any given hole, wouldn't hesitate to choose a perfect outcome rather than a perfect shot. He would prefer to be lucky than good.

So, with the greatest respect to Gary Player, it would seem the reporter was right. There is luck, always luck, when a golfer holes an iron shot – however hard he may have practised.

Part III

Witnesses

8

The new fate

I

In the middle of the twentieth century it was claimed that a new kind of fate had been discovered. It was not a shapely goddess or an agent of divine will. Its intentions were not revealed to oracles or soothsayers. It was blind to both superstition and prayer. It is arguably the most controversial and significant scientific breakthrough of the modern world, and I waited in London to meet the man who discovered it.

It is DNA, and the scientist who discovered its structure – alongside Francis Crick, Maurice Wilkins and Rosalind Franklin – is James Watson.

DNA has brought Watson considerable fame and occasional notoriety. Fortunately, there is no sign that either has made him guarded. That is unusual. Great men are often boring, not because they are conceited – though there is that, too – but because they become cautious. With nothing to gain and everything to lose, they avoid the risk of saying anything controversial. Instead, like royalty at a summer garden-party, great men are tempted to take refuge in banalities, dutifully patting the conversational ball over the net, happy to keep the rally wearily alive, but never injecting any spin, pace or fizz – and all the while hoping that you will eventually bow to the tedium and strike up a new rally elsewhere.

I hadn't reckoned on Watson, trenchant intellectual, Nobel Laureate and discoverer of the structure of DNA. I waited to meet him in the lounge of Brown's Hotel, a few hundred yards from Green Park. Watson duly arrived, wearing a green cashmere sweater that suggested the genteel atmosphere of a classy American country club, and skipped into the room with impressive energy for an eighty-one-year-old. He made straight towards me. And straight past me. The day's newspapers, in particular the *Financial Times*, arranged invitingly on the table just behind me, were obviously of greater immediate interest. It was done, I think, partly for effect. 'Old people are so dull,' he began, holding up the pink newspaper, 'because they're not doing anything new. I've stayed in intellectual life because I still read. If I didn't push new facts into my head, I would become duller and duller. So what you have *in* your head is just as important *as* your head. Breakfast?'

It was not a bad way to start an interview. As if to prove the point that he's still intellectually alert, he begins with a short disquisition on chance and the economy. 'The banks hired all these bright mathematicians who came out with statements like, "There's only a one-in-fifty chance that this can go wrong." But they never considered the one in fifty. It was just incredibly bad judgement. Economic theory is good for economists but bad for the banks.'

Watson is warming to the theme, all the more because it isn't *his* theme. 'Let's just *chat* for a while,' he says, initially waving away my tape recorder. Like a professional cricketer limbering up with a game of football before resuming the serious business of bat and ball, Watson likes discussing other disciplines first. Talking economics gives him an opportunity playfully to flex his muscles. 'Distribution is the big issue,' he continues, evidently unhappy about the vast wealth still being accrued by the elite of super-rich winners – and in particular their influence over President Obama's administration. 'The rich have seized control of the Democratic Party. The Democratic Party is the new Republican Party – and the Republican Party is a new fringe party … I need coffee!' Are external stimulants really necessary? If all this is before coffee, and within a few minutes of shaking hands, I am already confident that Watson was serious when he called his memoir *Avoid Boring People*.

In the past, Watson has certainly taken outspokenness too far. In 2007, during an interview with a friend, he dismissed the idea that 'equal powers of reason' were shared across racial groups. The remark inevitably sparked a massive backlash against Watson and prompted both an apology and his departure as Chancellor of the Cold Spring Harbor Laboratory. For all the offence the episode caused, the fact that Watson is still giving interviews now – even to strangers like me – is surely to his credit. Most other distinguished old men would have responded by retreating entirely into their shells.

If that incident made Watson temporarily infamous, his lasting fame derives from having discovered the structure of DNA. On 28 February 1953, Watson's colleague Francis Crick walked into the Eagle Pub in Cambridge and announced, 'We have found the secret of life.' They were, of course, right. The unearthing of the double-helix structure turned out to be one of the greatest scientific discoveries of the twentieth century and won them the 1962 Nobel Prize.

Was he lucky? Watson replies that it shouldn't have been his discovery to make. 'The luck was the other people. There was a three-person horse race and the two horses that should have won both stumbled.'

The 'two favourites' he is referring to were the American chemist Linus Pauling and the Austrian biochemist Erwin Chargaff. 'Pauling and Chargaff were on the same boat going back from an international biochemical conference in Paris. And they didn't like each other. If they'd just talked to each other over one meal, Pauling would have won [been the first to discover the structure of DNA]. If he'd just talked to Chargaff! It was pure luck.' Acknowledging the luck factor doesn't diminish Watson's evident delight. I sense he likes winning. 'One of my rules: never go into a field if there are more than three people in it! What's your chance if you're competing against twenty people, even if you're the best horse? Not good! So you should go into a field because it's going to become popular not because it's already popular.'

Then there was the role of Francis Crick. 'Another of my rules: never be the brightest person in the room. I didn't know any chemistry. So it was tremendous luck that I went to Cambridge and met Crick. But he was really misusing his time, he was doing worthless science ...' Watson repeats the phrase – '*worthless* science' – this time with heavy emphasis. 'Because he really didn't know enough biology to say "This is crap." So our meeting was, by most conventional things, real luck. I would never have succeeded if Francis hadn't been there. He certainly never would have found the structure – or even tried to find it – if I hadn't been there.'

He has been very gracious about Crick, but the famous Watson confidence quickly reasserts itself. 'Luck is the opportunity. But using it when you get an opportunity – that's just intelligence.'

If the partnership with Crick was lucky synergy, there was one moment of genuine serendipity. In mid-February 1953, as Watson and Crick circled around the discovery of DNA, they seemed to hit a brick wall. 'For two weeks I got nowhere.' Fortunately, Watson and Crick shared an office with Jerry Donahue, a young theoretical chemist from the California Institute of Technology on a six-month scholarship to Cambridge. Donahue informed Watson that the chemistry textbook he was using was incorrect. It was the final breakthrough.

'I changed the locations of the hydrogen atoms on my cardboard cut-outs of the molecules. The next morning, 28 February 1953, the key features of the DNA model all fell into place ...When Crick arrived, he took it all in rapidly, and gave my base-pairing schemes his blessing ...We felt sure this was it.' A few hours later, Crick made his 'secret of life' lunchtime announcement – and the two names became one of the most famous pairings in the history of science.

For Watson and Crick to be the first to discover the structure of DNA, they needed first to meet each other, then for Pauling and Chargaff to fluff their hand on that boat, and finally to work next to Donahue. There was one other stroke of luck Watson enjoys talking about. 'At that time, all I cared about was the DNA structure. It was aided by the fact that effectively there were no girls in Cambridge. I didn't think about men, so what do you think about? DNA. The Cambridge that exists now is a much harder place to do great science.'

II

The idea that genes constitute a version of fate long predates the discovery of the structure of DNA. From the beginning, the real science of genetics has, unfortunately for its reputation, overlapped with bogus science.

The first problem was explicitly political. Francis Galton, the infamous Victorian champion of the science of heredity also invented the politics of eugenics, tainting the whole subject of heredity from the start.

The second problem facing genetics was much more subtle. Genetics asks an impertinent and often disturbing question: how much of our character, health and intelligence is entirely beyond our control? To what extent do our genes constitute our fate?

It is not a question well suited to our times; it threatens our liberal faith in choice and self-determination. Jonathan Sacks, the British Chief Rabbi, summarized what most of us want to believe: 'Modernity is the transition from fate to choice.' Sacks meant that an individual can live a better life through his freedom to make choices. But the same logic applies to society at large. If humanity is malleable by nurture, then we can make a perfect, or at least very nearly perfect, social world. That notion – the *tabula rasa*, the blank slate – clearly dovetailed neatly with the liberal agenda of progressive egalitarianism. Nurture seemed optimistic and modern; genes were on the wrong side of history.

Watson identified that intellectual tension during our breakfast: 'People who don't like nature – the opposition from the left – want to blame everything on human frailty, and if humans were better then life would be better. But if your fate is determined by your genes, then you can't do anything about it.'

So genetics faced an uncomfortable paradox from the start. The ascent of knowledge usually implies human empowerment. Genetics cuts the other way: it threatens to subjugate human agency and undermines political idealism. Genetics, in that sense, was literally fated from the start.

Two of Watson's favourite words are 'boring', usually followed by a boyish grin, and 'bright', accompanied by an approving look. He clearly sees brightness as central to his way of looking at the world. I also sense, between the lines, that he believes intelligence to be largely innate. 'John McCain always wanted to be President. He was just too dumb to get there.' Watson giggles at the thought. 'If he was bright, he wouldn't have chosen Sarah Palin.' I take it that Watson thinks human destiny is more determined by the luck of your genes than by the serendipity of events. 'You could probably write about the chance that propelled Mrs Thatcher to 10 Downing Street,' he adds. 'But it wouldn't be the real story. The real story was she was an Iron Lady.' And where does that come from? 'I can't think of any place other than the genes.'

When Watson isn't talking about politics, he likes to use sporting analogies – particularly given his interviewer. He still plays a lot of tennis, and to a high standard. 'If I get the first piece ever about me as a sports jock, I'd be happy. You might think I'm trying to help mankind, but that's it really.' Later in the day, Roger Federer will play in yet another Grand Slam final. It reminds Watson that he owns two tennis rackets. One belonged to Federer. 'It's much lighter, with a smaller sweet-spot.' The second was once Rafael Nadal's – 'It's bigger and heavier,' he adds reproachfully. The implication, I think, is that Federer's racket requires superior talent because it's so hard to find the middle of the sweet spot.

Watson has one last parallel and he seems particularly pleased that he is saying it to a former cricketer. His eyes light up at a bespoke analogy he can't have used before: 'Do you have free will when a cricket ball is bowled at you? In fact, it's a very conditioned response. It's like a tennis return. There's almost no decision-making involved. You do not think through how you're going to do it.'

Yes, but you do have more choice when you serve. So does Watson think that the nature of life is like serving, or like returning, which flows along more preordained tracks? No prizes for guessing that he instinctively believes life is like returning serve. 'We like to believe it's like serving, but it's already pretty much encoded in your brain. You like to feel it's under your control. Not that it really is. Sometimes life is totally out of your control. You'd like to think that most of your life is controlled – that's almost essential to any successful life.'

But the scientist can't avoid saying what he believes to be true, however unsettling it might be: 'All we've done now is replace the gods with genes.'

III

It's rare to hear someone so admiring of genetic inheritance. The concept of innate talent – essentially an everyday synonym for evolutionary advantage – has been under attack in recent years. That is true in both sport and life. It is a striking fact that the more man has discovered about his genetic inheritance, the more determined he has become to deny its potency.

David Shenk's *The Genius in All of Us* told us that 'everything you've been told about genetics, talent and intelligence is wrong' – which presumes rather a lot not just about talent but also about the reader. Malcolm Gladwell's *Outliers* popularized the idea that practice, not talent, ultimately determines success. Matthew Syed's *Bounce* argued that geniuses – from Mozart to Federer – are 'made' rather than 'born'. And Dan Coyle's *The Talent Code* insisted that talent was a myth, a hoax, an old wives' tale. In fact, it was even worse than that: talent was a conspiracy.

One pillar of this line of argument is the psychologist Anders Ericsson. He claimed in a study of concert pianists that the 'talented' ones were less likely to reach the pinnacle of the classical music world than those who practised exceptionally hard. Ericsson's study has inspired a wave of books which maintain that talent is a myth. Success has a hidden logic, they say, a code that is equally available to all of us. Attacking talent has proved very popular on two fronts. First, it reflects well on those who have already triumphed, making success seem meritocratic and just. Secondly, it democratizes the future: success is open to anyone who puts in the hours.

Nurturists point to the example of the educational psychologist László Polgár. He publicly boasted, even before his children were born, that they would all become chess champions. He had three daughters, Susan, Sofia and Judit. Polgár was proved right. Susan became the top-rated female player in the world in 1984; Sofia once completed a remarkable streak of eight tournament victories; and Judit has been the world's number-one female chess player for over a decade.

I am not blind to the influence of nurture. My own research suggests that success is partly determined by socio-economic factors. As we've seen, a typical English professional cricket team today has a higher percentage of privately educated players than the same team did thirty years ago. I do, however, question the fundamental assumption made by some recent writers about talent, namely that the alleged predominance of nature over nurture represents the prevailing view. In fact, I would say nurturists, not genetic-determinists, are dominating the debate. It's not true that genetics is creating a culture of fatalism. Which of the following phrases have you heard more often? First: 'If you want something badly enough you can achieve it.' Or second: 'I'm precluded from doing this by my bad genes.'

I've encountered the first sentence infinitely more often than the second. Faith in nurture, not nature, is both more widely shared and more intellectually fashionable. If the truth lies somewhere between the two, then it is nature that needs to fight back, not nurture. So may I, as a non-scientist, provide three gentle counter-arguments, nudges that I hope will persuade you that innate talent does indeed exist?

First, and crucially, demonstrating that all champions spend thousands of hours practising does *not* prove that there is no such thing as a genetic element to sporting prowess. It is a reductive error of logic. Practice is necessary, but it is not sufficient on its own. We could fill thousands of pages with examples of *failed* sportsmen – or musicians and actors – who spent thousands of hours practising and yet did not succeed in making the top grade.

Nor does dedicated practice explain what separates geniuses from their nearest rivals. The best 1,000 ballerinas in the world are all slim and disciplined. So we can be confident that slimness and discipline differentiate all 1,000 dancers from a randomly selected group of people we round up on the street. But that does not prove, or come close to proving, that diet and exercise differentiate the world's very *best* ballerina from the other 999 merely excellent dancers. If it did, in a world as competitive as modern dance, wouldn't the other 999 just slavishly copy her training methods?

When Usain Bolt broke the world record in the 100 metres, he ran it in 9.58 seconds, beating Tyson Gay (who ran 9.71) into second place. That difference, 0.13 of a second, means that Bolt was about 1.3 per cent better than Gay. What explains Bolt being 1.3 per cent better than Gay? Is it that the famously relaxed Usain Bolt practises 1.3 per cent more than Gay? Or is that they both practise optimally, and Bolt is simply 1.3 per cent more talented than Gay? I know which one I would put my money on.

Matthew Syed is a colleague at *The Times* whom I admire and respect. But it would be dishonest of me to deny that I disagree with his theory that geniuses are genetically no different from the rest of us. He argues in *Bounce*: 'It is

Federer's regular practice that has given him his advantage, not his genes ... Top performers are not born with sharper instincts, they possess enhanced awareness and anticipation ... The key thing to note is that these cannot possibly be innate skills. Federer did not come into the mortal world with knowledge of where to look or how to efficiently extract information on a service return.' It is true that no one thinks that there is a 'tennis gene' waiting to be discovered. But that does not mean that Roger Federer's genes have no part to play in his excellence on the tennis court.

My own experience convinces me that innate ability certainly exists. I played professional cricket with and against players who I thought were simply more talented than I was. What do I mean by that? You learn a lot about pure talent when you watch sportsmen try out new disciplines. Professional cricketers often have fun together by playing other sports, and, inevitably, it was hard to find a sport that everyone had played when they were growing up – West Indians had never played rugby before, Englishmen didn't have any experience of Australian Rules Football.

But I learned that the most talented sportsmen, those with exceptional innate athletic talent, could almost instantly pick up games that were entirely new to them. One team-mate, who had never played rugby before, quicky became a stand-out player. He had a brilliant intuitive sense of space, an instinct of where the gaps would be and how to exploit them. He could escape and elude tacklers as though he had been playing rugby all his life. Practice? He'd never played the game before. It was talent.

That is the type of aptitude Roger Federer has for tennis. He then honed his talent over many thousands of hours of practice. Result: optimal talent plus superb nurture equals sixteen grand slams. In fact, the sports scientist and rugby coach Simon Worsnop used Federer as the perfect example of innate ability to answer the 'talent is a myth' approach:

> Roger Federer's great, great etc. grandfather has very good anticipation of movement of wild animals and has a great capacity to learn these; because of this he is able to hunt successfully, not to get eaten and successfully pass on his genes to numerous offspring. After the first agrarian revolution Roger's ancestor lived in a small village and tended his crops and these genes no longer offered a selective advantage. But they were still there. Many generations later they offer an advantage within sport when subjected to 'similar' stresses and stimulations that they faced many thousands of years ago.

Rafael Nadal, his great rival, tried to capture that same truth about Federer: 'His physique – his DNA – seems perfectly adapted to tennis. You get these blessed freaks of nature in other sports too.' That is not a proof, of course. It is a hypothesis. But it is a hypothesis that almost everyone who has played sport would recognize as being highly likely. And there is no scientific evidence I know of that disproves what common sense holds to be true: that it takes the perfect combination of practice *and* genes to become the very best.

Sadly, many modern professional sportsmen are reluctant to admit that they have innate gifts. It sounds arrogant, and it robs them of meritocratic approval for having earned their triumphs through hard work alone. This reluctance is seized on by writers advocating nurture as evidence that there is no such thing as talent. They like to pile up personal story after personal story of quotes from winners and champions. You know the kind of quotes. 'I practised till mum came out and dragged me in for dinner ... I wasn't very talented, I just worked harder at my game ... I'd kick that ball until I had calluses all over my feet ... I wasn't very talented ... Hunger was my secret weapon.'

Sometimes it is the friends of brilliant sportsmen who downplay talent. At a dinner for Shane Warne, I heard one of Britain's leading interviewers say that what set Warne apart from normal human beings was simple: he practised more. With respect to both Warne and the speaker, from what I saw of the great bowler – whether it was before, during or after matches – I'd say he was sometimes out-practised by more willing time-servers, but never trumped in terms of talent, competitiveness or self-belief. There's no crime in that, is there?

But some people do see talent as a cause of reproach. That is why a sportsman's attitude towards it changes during his career. When you're young, you want to be thought of as talented. You want to be an exciting talent, a thrilling prospect, a force of nature. When you're established – when there is a body of evidence to judge you by – that changes. I saw a disruptive senior player constantly undermine a captain by beginning each sentence to him with the phrase, 'Don't you think, given all your natural talent . . .' What he meant was that the captain was an underachiever (he wasn't, by the way).

A disruptive player I had to captain used to say the same about me. He would pepper his conversation with little put-downs, 'With your talent . . . the way you strike the ball . . . when it comes as easily as . . .' The implication was that I had got through on talent, that I hadn't worked at it, that I'd coasted (not true, either – I wasn't that good).

So we end up with a distinctly weird paradox. In prospect, talent is a good thing to have. In retrospect, it is almost a guilty secret. Champions have a vested interest in denying talent. That's why there is a narrative bias in favour of nurture. Most testimony from successful people is drawn from inter-views after they have retired. I question its legitimacy. There is a natural impulse – after the event – to attribute success to hard work rather than ability. It fits our meritocratic faith in just deserts. It suits the industriousness of the professional era. And it appeals to the audience: they can do it, too.

If you asked great men and women when they were twenty what set them apart from the crowd you would get a different answer from the weary clichés they trot out at forty or sixty. I bet, aged twenty, more would say they had the raw talent to go all the way. I'd trust the hungry kid who speaks before he thinks, not the great man with one eye on posterity.

IV

I think the influence of talent in sport is set to increase rather than diminish. It's to do with globalization and professionalism. If that sounds vague, let me elaborate.

Globalization has affected sport more quickly and more deeply than almost any other sphere. It is undermining our old clichés about sport and nationality. Globalization hasn't merely brought the same T-shirts to sportsmen all around the world. It has also propagated, in each sport, a dominant style of play. We are now part of a worldwide sporting community, not just a national or local one.

As a consequence, old national traits are dying out. Cricketers once spoke about Indian batsmanship in cricket, a distinct branch of the discipline, one that had been honed on dusty, spinning wickets, a style of play based on deft touches rather than brute power. Above all, Indian batsmanship was passed on from generation to generation, a unique pairing of textbook orthodoxy and delicate wristiness.

India are still a skilled batting team. But they now bat much more like the stars from other countries. The muscular batting of M. S. Dhoni, the Indian cricket captain, is radically different from the old-fashioned caricature of Indian batsmanship. England's opening batsmen, Alastair Cook and Andrew Strauss, are both back-foot specialists, happier hooking and cutting than driving. If you didn't know better, you could easily assume that they had learnt to bat on the sun-baked bouncy pitches of Australia, rather than the damp grass of Oxfordshire and Bedford.

What has happened here? How did batting style become globalized? It's a combination of the influence of TV, player movement and international coaching. And it has affected every sport, not only cricket.

First, satellite television has homogenized sporting style. Kids can choose to play like any international stars, not simply copy their local heroes. Unsurprisingly, they choose to bat like the best in the world, not the best in their own country. For example, when I played in India in 2002, the England batsman Michael Vaughan was ranked number one in the world and the Indian kids I met were all copying him as they watched him smash Australia on their satellite TVs. The same pick-and-choose philosophy happens everywhere. You can select a batting hero from anywhere in the world – India, Australia, England, wherever – and choose to model your game on him.

The growing homogeneity of cricket techniques is shared by other international sports. Players move around much more. There is a global marketplace for international sportsmen. Football is obviously the most complete and fluid world marketplace, but almost every major sport now has an international job market. I played professional cricket in the same team as Sri Lankans, Indians, Australians, West Indians, Zimbabweans, South Africans, Irishmen and Dutchmen. As players from different countries routinely play alongside each other at club level, learning new tricks and exchanging ideas, the differences between their sporting cultures gradually diminishes.

Coaches are as mobile as players. I was coached by as many different nationalities as I played alongside. The days when coaches were drawn from the native population are over. A successful professional sports coach today can expect to ply his trade all over the world. Coaching has become an international business, and a band of elite coaches, drawn from a broad range of countries, spreads ideas around the world. In the last few years, Chelsea FC alone has been managed by two Italians, two Portuguese, a Brazilian and an Israeli. A new lingua franca of tactics and training methods has arisen internationally.

How does this affect the importance of talent? Look at the 2010 football World Cup. The paucity of goals baffled many onlookers. The explanation is simple: established coaches from old-world football nations had taught newer, previously less well-drilled teams how to organize themselves. Footballing knowledge had spread around the world. The most marked change was improved defence. Why? Because defence is relatively easy to learn, as it relies on organization; attack is difficult to teach because it relies on flair. If your defence is well coached, you can learn to nullify a better team. At the very worst, you can reduce the margin of defeat. The internationalization of coaching has made it harder to score goals.

Having increasingly well-organized teams, as we saw at the World Cup, certainly reduces the gap between the best and the worst. As it gets harder to break down international defences, you need more talented attacking players to do it. As coaching homogenizes defence, talent – which cannot be coached – will become the differentiating factor. Notice that Spain won the World Cup. It is significant that they benefited from an abundance of talented players in the crucial play-maker positions: not only Xavi and Iniesta (whose goal won the final), but also Cesc Fabregas (who came on as replacement and set up the Iniesta goal).

The 2010 tournament was dominated by defence. And yet the most talented team (in my opinion) won it. It is a paradox of nature and nurture we will see increasingly often in professional sport: as the well-drilled strategies cancel each other out, then attacking talent will become an increasingly decisive factor.

I think tennis is following a similar trend. In 1986, 1987, 1988 and 1989 Ivan Lendl was the world's top-ranked tennis player. Lendl dragged himself to the top more through willpower and hard work than natural talent. He famously took preparation to a new level. He hired the same workers who laid the hardcourt surfaces at Flushing Meadows – the court where he reached eight successive US Open finals – to install an exact copy in the grounds of his home in Greenwich, Connecticut.

In the 1980s, such planning was unheard of in a sport that was only just coming to terms with the outer limits of practice and dedication. The Lendl approach has been copied by his successors. Now all major players train specifically on the surface they are about to compete on. Not, admittedly, in their own homes. But when you can get to the right court anywhere in the world on your own jet, why spoil the garden?

Paradoxically, Lendl's example will not help future players in the Lendl mould. Why? As the training methods of *every* top tennis player improve, it gets harder to find an edge through practice. When everyone gets better at practice, talent inevitably becomes a more decisive factor. That's good news for international tennis; bad news for players who don't have as much talent as their competitors. The result is that it will become rarer for players such as Ivan Lendl to dominate world tennis. Recent history suggests that this is already happening. It is Roger Federer – regarded by his peers and rivals as freakily talented – who has accumulated a world record sixteen grand slams over the last decade.

Yes, Federer practises very hard. But few observers believe it is practice that sets him apart. After all, almost *everyone* now practises hard. There's nothing else to do as a professional sportsman. So it is getting more difficult to become the best in the world primarily through work ethic. As an explanation of outcomes, practice is running out of steam. Federer is often considered a throwback to an older age of grace and elegance. In fact, the Federer type of champion is likely to dominate the future of sport. As training methods become ever more scientific, talent will increasingly separate the best from the rest. There will be more Federers at the top, fewer Lendls.

Logic supports my hunch. Imagine a world in which practice was absolutely forbidden. There would be no way of battling to achieve excellence through hard work because hard work had been banned. In such a world, when no one does any practice at all, talent will determine who wins. In the absence of any divergence in nurture, nature will determine the outcome.

Now imagine a world in which all the competitors practise equally well and equally hard. In this imagined scenario, talent will *still* determine who wins. In a world in which environmental conditions are identical, when all competitors practise optimally, genes will determine the outcome because nurture has now been *cancelled out*.

In other words, the influence of practice is shaped like a bell-curve. It is zero at both extremes: when no one practises, or when everyone practises optimally. It is highest in the middle, where the *divergence* in the methods of practice is the greatest.

The early years of professional sport – what we have just lived through – will be remembered as the high point of divergence in practice methods. Think of the evolution of modern sport. There was enormous potential to gain a competitive advantage through practice. That is exactly what happened in the early history of professional sport. Training methods improved dramatically; athletes dedicated their whole lives to their sport; diet became regulated and controlled; sportsmen became machines geared only towards winning. Teams that embraced advanced training methods earlier – because they were richer or more dedicated, or both – gained a massive advantage over their more old-fashioned and talent-dependent rivals. Nurture was in the ascendant.

And it was undoubtedly mostly nurture, not nature, that led world records to be smashed so comprehensively in the early decades of professional athletics. The first modern marathon, at the 1896 Olympic Games, was won by Spiridon Lousi, a Greek water-carrier, in just under three hours. Today's world record, held by Haile Gebrselassie, is 2 hours, 3 minutes and 59 seconds. In a little over a century, man has become a third quicker – an improvement that cannot be explained by snail-paced evolutionary advances in genetic talent.

But look more carefully at the world-record times: we are now *inching* towards progress, not bounding. Human beings cannot continue to improve indefinitely at the rapid rate of the early decades of professionalism. As I explored in *What Sport Tells Us About Life*, if we want to feel really gloomy, we should consider the plight of animals. Racehorses stopped getting faster years ago. Humans, too, will also soon begin approaching what Stephen Jay Gould called 'the outer wall of human endeavour'.

So, as they get closer, inching towards ever more scientific athletic brilliance, put your money on talent, not practice. After all, practice is only the determining factor between athletes when it is significantly varied – varied enough to trump the difference in talent. But if everyone practises iden-tically and optimally – and professional sport is moving rapidly towards that situation – then the restoration of talent as the critical factor will be complete.

Consider what science tells us about heritability in the non-sporting world. A good example is myopia (nearsightedness). The heritability of myopia is low in semi-literate societies, because your myopia is partly determined by whether you learn to read (close focusing causes myopia, but only in some susceptible people). Once everybody learns to read, the myopia becomes a largely heritable condition because all those who are gentically susceptible will have it. The more nurture you provide, the more nature differentiates.

So Jim Watson may yet be granted his wish to be regarded as a sage of the sporting world. Genetic fate? That's certainly too strong a word. But don't expect the dumb luck of your genes to diminish in importance any time soon. We will doubtless cling to the idea that the ball is in our court and that it is our turn to serve. But, in truth, the destiny of the ball was determined – at least in part – long before we had the chance even to lay our racket on it.

9

Fooled by Randomness revisited

I conclude, therefore, that as fortune is changeable whereas men are obstinate in their ways, men prosper so long as fortune and policy are in accord, and when there is a clash they fail.

Niccolò Machiavelli, *The Prince* (trans. George Bull)

I

There aren't many advantages in having your ankle immobilized in a huge plastic moon-boot. You can't exercise properly, but unfortunately you can consume the same amount of calories just as easily. And you can't influence events on the field, but you can still worry about them.

There is only one definite advantage: you do have time to read. One book, in particular, has stayed with me from that frustratingly stationary summer. It was given to me by a thoughtful Middlesex supporter while I was hobbling around the Lord's pavilion. It was *Fooled by Randomness*, the book that made the trader turned author Nassim Taleb into the world's most famous scourge of the banking system. It's quite a tribute to Middlesex fans, really. Where else but at Lord's would an injured sportsman get a gift like that?

I knew about Taleb, but I'd never read him. The previous summer, I had been asked to review Taleb's subsequent book, *The Black Swan*, about the impact of highly improbable events. But I had been flat out captaining Middlesex and had to decline. Now, a year on and with my ankle in a cast, I had more than enough time on my hands. You could say it took *my* black swan to find Taleb's.

I arranged to meet up with Taleb, and the day we chose, weeks in advance, was 10 October. Bizarrely, that turned out to be Black Friday, the eye of the financial storm. As the banking system tottered on the brink of collapse, Taleb's stock rose – no wonder he couldn't resist the occasional glance towards his BlackBerry. I was interviewing a theorist of chance and randomness on the very day, randomly selected, that he described, only partly exaggerating, as 'the most important day of his life'.

Taleb's manner is kinder in person than that of the narrator he cultivates in his books. But his conversation captures exactly the same mixture of combativeness, amusement and wry disbelief. I expect he would wholeheartedly agree with the classical maxim, 'More enemies, more honour.'

The timing of *The Black Swan*, perfectly in sync with the financial crisis, undoubtedly made Taleb's name. But though

The Black Swan caused a bigger splash, *Fooled by Randomness* left a greater impression on me.

Fooled by Randomness explores two questions that had preoccupied me in my sports career. The first is the general problem of causality. Taleb cheerfully told me he hates sport. But the insights of *Fooled by Randomness* are as applicable to sport as they are to finance.

Sport is full of the abject misunderstanding of causes. In particular, there is a never-ending quest to identify the wrong causes and pin them to the wrong events. Take that ever-green source of football legend, the half-time team-talk. This is wheeled out every time a football match undergoes a transformation after the half-time break. If Arsenal go into half-time 2–0 down, and score two goals in the second half, we are told by the commentators that 'Arsène Wenger's half-time team-talk really did the trick.' (Wenger, by the way, says very little to his players at half-time.) Clearly, there was a team-talk, and clearly there was a recovery. There is, however, no evidence that the former caused the latter.

The truth about team-talks, in all sports, is that the overwhelming majority of them make no impact whatsoever. They are not meant for the players, who very rarely listen to them anyway. They are meant for coaches so that they can cling to the illusion of control. A team-talk is not a strategic device. It's a set of rosary beads, something for the coach to do with his voice while he has a captive audience.

How, then, do we explain games that radically change direction in mid-match? By the law of averages, a large number of matches must inevitably change their shape some-where around the half-time mark. Goals have to be scored at some point, and those that randomly happen just after half-time are said to be 'caused' by the manager's half-time talk.

The same principle applies in another sphere where randomness is routinely misinterpreted as skill – the practice field. Imagine a typical training-ground scene: hot, tired players going through practice drills under the watchful eyes of a coach. Two players, in particular, are being put through their paces on a fielding drill. The first player carries out the task brilliantly first time, so the coach praises him extrava-gantly. And yet at the next attempt, perhaps with the praise ringing in his ears, the player performs the practice drill poorly. In contrast, the second player fails woefully first time. So the coach shouts abuse at him, and – whipped back into line – the player performs it infinitely better second time. The lesson is obvious. Praise makes players soft. Criticism makes them perform better.

That was the argument made by a coach to the psychology professor Daniel Kahneman. The coach instructed Israeli air pilots, not sportsmen, though that makes no difference to the general principle. It provided the spark for a theme that ran through Kahneman's career and ended with him winning the Nobel Prize for Economics in 2002.

Kahneman instinctively disagreed with the pilot instructor because he felt that reward generally works better than punishment. But how could he explain the experiences of his interviewee? The answer, Kahneman found, was that the screaming preceded the improvement, but it didn't cause it. In a series of repeated tasks, an extraordinary event is most likely to be followed, due purely to chance, by a more ordinary one. The phenomenon is called 'regression to the mean' and was neatly summarized by the physicist Leonard Mlodinow in *A Drunkard's Walk*:

> If a pilot made an exceptionally good landing – one far above his normal level of performance – then the odds would be good that he would perform closer to his norm – that is, worse – the next day. And if his instructor had praised him, it would appear that the praise had done him no good. But if a pilot made an exceptionally bad landing ... then the odds would be good that the next day he would perform closer to his norm – that is, better. And if his instructor had a habit of screaming 'you clumsy ape' when a student performed poorly, it would appear that his criticism did some good. In this way an apparent pattern would emerge: students perform well, praise no good; student performs poorly, instructor compares student to lower primate at high volume, student improves. The instructors in Kahneman's class had concluded from such experiences that their screaming was a powerful educational tool. In reality it made no difference at all.

If we understood randomness better, the logic follows, we would be simultaneously better teachers and kinder people. Perhaps, when an aggressive coach was abusing me for failing to master a practice drill, I should have told him to shut up and read up on Kahneman's theory of regression to the mean. No, you're right, that wouldn't have been a great career move.

Then there is the media. Taleb recounts a story from December 2003, when Saddam Hussein was captured. At first, Bloomberg News flashed the headline: 'U.S. treasury bonds rise; Hussein capture may not curb terrorism'. Half an hour later, as US treasury bonds fell in price, Bloomberg News ran the headline: 'U.S. treasuries fall; Hussein capture boosts allure of risky assets'. The same 'cause' (the capture of Saddam Hussein) was being stretched to explain one event (bonds go up) and its exact opposite (bonds go down).

Taleb should definitely stay away from the sports media, a sector of journalism even more resistant to the principle of randomness. My favourite dodgy 'cause' is 'off-field happiness'.

When a player beats his arch-rival to win a title, we read the following day that the critical factor in his success was the love of his family and the stability of his coaching staff. One month later, when he loses to the same opponent, we read that the critical factor was his *rival's* loving family and stable coaching staff. It is not, it must be said, terribly difficult to sustain this kind of writing. You can keep the template of the article the same, and just swap the names around.

There is, of course, a simpler explanation: it's the losing that makes you look rattled and lonely, not your girlfriend. The 'cause' is in fact a consequence of losing. But it takes a brave reporter to admit that we don't know exactly what explained a particular victory, or indeed if anything caused it.

Thinking about randomness in sport also led me to some awkward conclusions as a captain. If a difficult and disruptive team-mate went through a good spell, and someone congratulates you for 'managing him well', what should you do? If a captain tells the truth – 'I doubt I've had any influence on him at all because his behaviour is random and unpredictable' – then you risk sounding surly and aloof. But if you accept the credit, you risk reinforcing a correlation that doesn't really exist. When the difficult player reverts to type, as you suspect he will, you'll be saddled with the blame for *not* managing him well.

II

Is there any way of measuring these hypotheses? Is there a more rigorous way of demonstrating that randomness is a major factor in sport? Fortunately, the mathematician Brian Burke has done just that on his website 'Advanced NFL Stats'. Don't worry, you don't need any maths at all to follow his logic.

First, Burke imagined a world in which every sports match was determined entirely by pure chance. Instead of playing a match, there is just a flip of a fair coin. What would the National Football League table look like at the end of the season, when every team had 'played' its sixteen games?

As you would expect, eight wins and eight losses is the most common season outcome. About 20 per cent of all teams would finish eight–eight . About 5 per cent of all teams would finish with eleven wins and five losses and another 5 per cent would finish with five wins and eleven losses. Figure 2 shows how it looks on a graph.

Figure 2

Pure Luck

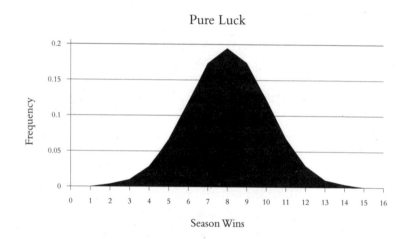

But to fans and pundits Burke goes on to explain: 'It would still appear that some teams are "better" than others. Some teams would even appear "hot" because they won several games in row, when in reality it's just an artifact of luck ...' Burke mocks knee-jerk punditry by asking: 'Does the coin have momentum? Is it hot?'

Now comes the fun part. Burke asks how a set of results

from a real NFL season compares to this imagined coin-toss league table. The graph in Figure 3 shows the distribution of the actual NFL regular-season wins for every team from 2002 to 2006 (a sample of 160 matches).

Figure 3

Actual 2002–2006

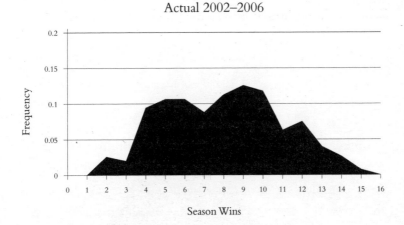

Season Wins

So how do the actual league results differ from the coin-toss league results? They are different, inevitably. But to what degree? Burke transposed the two as in Figure 4.

Burke concludes: 'By comparing the two distributions, we can calculate that of the 160 season outcomes, only 78 of them differ from what we'd expect from a pure luck distribution. That's only 48%, which would suggest that in 52% of NFL games, luck is the deciding factor!'

Figure 4

Actual / Luck

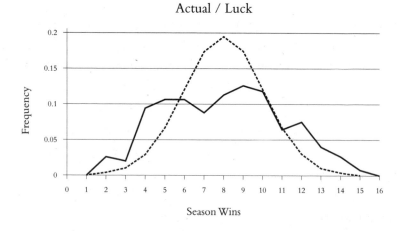

Initially Burke found it hard to accept his own logic. 'Frankly, I didn't buy it.' But he kept at it, and devised a more complex series of calculations that I'm happy – if you are – to take on trust. He concludes that his maths was right all along: an NFL match is determined roughly half by skill and half by randomness.

Imagine it. *Half* of what pundits, coaches and fans are trying to account for and understand is in fact impossible to understand or account for because it is determined by pure chance. Wouldn't it be delicious if a coach, in response to an aggressive fan or interviewer, replied that the real difference between this season and last season was pure luck?

III

Fooled by Randomness touched another raw nerve. The idea that we dress up luck as judgement or skill was a painful one to contemplate. When things are going well, it's not easy to say you've just been lucky. Between July 2000 and May 2008 I didn't miss a single game of first-class cricket through being dropped or being injured. To my superstitious father's dismay, I mentioned those facts when I was interviewed by a newspaper (he would call that tempting fate).

Was my unbroken sequence luck or resilience? I take some credit for the form part of the sequence. But not so much when it comes to the injury-free part. Batting is not particularly wearing: injuries tend to be externally caused, like broken fingers, rather than wear-and-tear injuries that can be managed by a dedicated fitness regime. So an injury to a batsman is usually a case of luck rather than negligence. Sitting with my ankle in a cast, I was starting to understand that I hadn't been the sole determining factor in my unbroken sequence of games.

It's one of Taleb's themes: what looks like a great track record is sometimes just a lucky streak about to run out. 'In all my experience, I have never been in any accident. I never saw a wreck and never have been wrecked nor was I ever in any predicament that threatened to end in disaster of any sort.' That observation, written in 1907, came from the pen of E. J. Smith. Five years later, he was captain of the *Titanic* when it sank, killing 1,517 people.

Why does it matter if we often mistake judgement for luck, if we are fooled by randomness, if the world is steered more by the winds and the weather than it is by the captain's sagacity? The moral implications of that question bring us back to Taleb's central focus – the financial system. There are already more than enough books about the financial crisis. This isn't about to become another one.

But it is revealing that the financial crisis has continued to be dominated by arguments about luck. Even in early 2011, three and a half years after the collapse of Northern Rock, Ed Miliband wrote an article arguing that the previous Labour government was exceptionally unfortunate, a victim of deplorable financial luck. He was arguing that the electorate, spurred on by Tory lies, unfairly judged Brown's economic record at the 2010 general election. The nub of his case was this: the credit crunch was an international crisis that hobbled Labour's otherwise sound stewardship of the economy. Gordon Brown, by implication, was simply the unluckiest Prime Minister who ever lived: a great leader who was the victim of events as an unforeseeable financial crisis cruelly wrecked a blameless economic record. The desertion of Labour at the subsequent election was *unjust*.

Miliband is certainly right in one sense. Academic research supports the idea that voters often can't tell the difference between lucky governments and skilful ones. Andrew Leigh, an economist at the Australian National University, studied 268 elections held across the world between 1978 and 1999.

Leigh's research evaluates how much a country's economic performance is due to booms in the world economy (what Leigh calls 'luck'), and how much is attributable to good government ('competence') – and whether voters can tell the difference.

Let's take lucky governments first. Being in office during a world boom means you're significantly more likely to be re-elected. A government's average rate of re-election is 57 per cent. But when world growth is 1 percentage point above normal, the government's re-election rate jumps to a 64 per cent likelihood. Effectively, voters endorse the ship that is raised by a tide beyond the captain's control – and a lucky Prime Minister benefits from an unearned 7 per cent boost to his electoral chances.

What about 'competence': how do voters reward governments that outperform the rest of the world? It is more important to be a lucky government than an effective government. Even superb economic management, outpacing world growth by 1 percentage point, only raises the Prime Minister or President's likelihood of re-election from 57 per cent to 60. An economically competent government gets an electoral boost of 3 per cent; a lucky one gets a leg up of 7 per cent. Competence, Leigh concludes, is barely half as effective as luck.

Napoleon demanded lucky generals. All that politicians need is a (global) boom. 'It's the economy, stupid,' was the message of James Carville's famous memo to Bill Clinton's election team in 1992. True to the Clinton team's logic,

President Bush was indeed blamed for the recession in America and Clinton was elected in his place.

Events which, in hindsight, we regard as inevitable, frequently entailed a hefty slice of luck. It is easy to forget – given Barack Obama's huge and historic victory in November 2008 – that John McCain was ahead in the polls before Lehman Brothers collapsed in September 2007. No one could claim that macro-economics was McCain's strong suit, and Obama's electoral fortunes were clearly boosted by attention shifting to the collapse of the US economy. (Ironically, as President he has been hamstrung by it.)

Tony Blair, with the easy good grace of someone who walked away before a catastrophe, acknowledged his economic luck in a speech at Yale University shortly after he resigned. It was hard not to admire his admission that he had been very lucky to be Prime Minister during a period of world economic growth. (Curious he did not do so while still in office.)

So was Gordon Brown's Labour another of Leigh's unlucky governments? Was it simply unfortunate, as Miliband argued, that the credit crunch came while it was in power? Economic busts, after all, are a recurring fact of political life.

Unfortunately, Labour's rhetoric in office is somewhat at odds with their subsequent rhetoric of self-exculpation. Almost throughout his thirteen years as Chancellor and Prime Minister, the phrase 'No more boom and bust' was Gordon Brown's favourite mantra. It started in 1997 in his first pre-budget report when he 'put an end to the damaging cycle of boom and bust'. In the 2006 budget he promised 'No return to boom and bust'. And in his last budget as Chancellor, he reprised the pledge: 'We will never return to the old boom and bust.'

Revealingly, when asked during the credit crunch if he regretted his long-standing repetition of 'no more boom and bust', Brown denied he had even said it. The historical inaccuracy is one thing. The nature of Brown's preferred version is even more revealing: 'I actually said, "No more Tory boom and bust."' We can only conclude from this bizarre tribal climb-down that a Labour boom and bust is fine.

The wider point is that in boom years, we heard a lot from Brown about 'No more Tory boom and bust'. When the crash came, we heard a great deal about forces beyond his control, about an economic crisis that began in America, about contagion that crossed the Atlantic and infected the British economy. Perhaps, as many people suggested, Brown had the mindset and capacity for denial of an international financier all along. When the economy was going well, it was good judgement; when the economy crashed, it was just bad luck.

IV

The same narrative is repeated elsewhere in financial meltdowns. Good outcomes are dressed up as strategic strokes of genius; catastrophes are attributed to bad luck. We have already encountered the case of Long Term Capital Management and the economists who believed they had replaced mere gambling with hard science. You no longer needed luck to make lots of money, they said. You just needed the Black-Scholes formula.

LTCM went catastrophically bust in 1998. After its collapse, LTCM partner Eric Rosenfeld explained away his fund's epic failure with the argument that unique events had conspired against them: 'I do think it was something that never happened before.'

Even after the financial crisis of 2007–9, Myron Scholes deflected blame. When he was asked if his models were partly responsible, Scholes replied – apparently without irony – that it was just bad luck. His formula had simply been misused by inept bankers: 'Sometimes you can build a wonderful car, such as a Porsche or a Lamborghini, and then turn it over for someone to drive who has no skills who causes it to crash or fail' – neatly ignoring his own track record behind the wheel. Myron Scholes's 'Lady Fortuna' defence became a recurring theme of the financial crisis. Northern Rock's CEO Adam Applegarth argued that there was nothing he could have done to avoid the run on his bank. Summoned by the House of Commons Treasury Select Committee, Applegarth claimed that it was extraordinarily bad luck. The culprit was Lady Fortuna, not Adam Applegarth. Dick Fuld, CEO of Lehman Brothers, made a similar case to an American Congressional committee. 'I wake up *every single night* thinking, "What could I have done differently? What could I have said? What should I have done?'" But Fuld was unable to think of anything he *could* have done differently. Human skill was hopeless in the face of such odds stacked against him.

Would Fuld or Applegarth or Scholes have advanced the same argument during the boom years? That leadership and decision-making had little to do with their firms' profits, that managerial capability was scarcely the point, that it was simply the luck of benevolent economic conditions, a rising tide that raised all ships? Has any Fuld-type banker ever made the case that profits were merely the accidental by-products of a fortuitous financial climate, that it was just a good run while it lasted, that he was simply lucky to hold office at the right time?

No, because his position and astronomic salary would become instantly untenable and unjustifiable. But when fortune was reversed, when his luck ran out, Fuld played the fate card. On the way up, it was him (skill). On the way down it was them (forces beyond his control). That really is a case of 'Tails I win, heads you lose'.

10

Accidents 1

I

From my early days at Cambridge, spent alternating between the cricket ground Fenner's and the University Library, I have shuttled gratefully between history and sport. Sometimes it has been hard to reconcile the two. In my thirteen years as a professional cricketer, one question frequently asked of me, and not always in the most diplomatic language, was whether a degree in history had any practical benefits. Why, my dressing-room inquisitor would wonder, should we pay all this tax to send people like you to study things that happened hundreds of years ago?

It's a fair question. Every sportsman has an uneasy relationship with history, even with his own memory. There is so much you have to forget in sport. A cricketer who walks to the batting crease with an encyclopaedic grasp of all his batting failures is very likely soon to add another to his sequence. Experience can be harder to handle than innocence, and most spells of bad form in sport would be greatly helped by a magic pill containing nothing stronger than temporary amnesia. I know I often wished I was more like a goldfish and less like a historian.

Faced with these demons of the past, it isn't hard to see why many sportsmen cultivate an aggressively forward-thinking philosophy. Far better to keep rolling ever onwards, from pitch to bar, and then from bar to pitch – without pausing for thought in case they paralyse themselves with self-doubt.

The study of the past seems alien to the sporting mindset, alien perhaps to the practical temperament in general. Playing sport is an endless schedule of future battles, campaigns yet to begin, stories awaiting a shape. Like actors, most sportsmen can only bear so much introspection, and so much is very little. Why, when there are so many 'real' events looming around the corner – plans to be drawn up, tactics to settle upon – should we waste time and energy in irrelevant backwaters where events can no longer be influenced?

History and sport: one a study of what has already happened, the second the execution of the here and now. They are apparently opposites – the former requiring us to resuscitate the past, the second ephemeral, grasped only momentarily as we play, before slipping away into broken dreams and piles of yesterday's forgotten newspapers.

In one crucial respect, however, the study of history has overlapped with my life in sport. In fact, sometimes I am not sure if it is the history that has taught me about sport or the sport that has taught me about history. Breaking my ankle was just one further example that cemented the idea in my mind. It is that accidents matter far more than planning.

II

On 13 December 1931, an English politician – perhaps forgetting that American cars drive on the right-hand side of the road – was knocked down on New York's Fifth Avenue. The car was travelling at 35 miles per hour, more than fast enough to kill him. The politician was dragged several yards before being flung to one side. The veteran MP was fifty-seven years old and surely past the prime of his career.

What would his obituaries have said of his life and work? His political record was mixed. He had struggled to find either a political party or a stable constituency seat. Having failed to become an MP in 1899, he won a seat the following year, only to be disowned by his party for disloyalty three years later. In 1906, representing a different party, he won a new seat only to lose it again in 1908. Between 1922 and 1924 he campaigned three times to rejoin the House of Commons, fighting each election under a different political umbrella. He succeeded in returning to front-line politics in 1924, and a year later rejoined the party that had expelled him in 1903.

The year 1931 saw his political ambitions fall to a particularly low ebb. He had found an international cause – British rule in India – to excite him, but it had served mainly to alienate him from the leader of his party. Nor was it a brave stand to be proud of. History proved him to be on the wrong side of the argument: his position was anti-democratic and anachronistic at best, downright racist at worst.

He was a prolific journalist and author, but certainly not above churning out hack work just to pay the bills. He occasionally apologized for his tone, hoping the essays he wrote at the time of the accident would not be taken as 'merely the amusing speculations of a dilettante Cassandra'.

His military career was uneven, too. His courage was never in doubt; his judgement was. By far the most ambitious and influential military intervention of his career had ended in disaster and resignation. He reflected afterwards, 'I was ruined for the time being ... and a supreme enterprise was thrown away, through my trying to carry out a major and combined operation of war from a subordinate position.'

Public reversals were matched by recurrent financial worries. He was good at making money but even better at spending it. The 1929 stock-market crash hit him particularly hard, forcing him to close his country house and retreat with his family into a cottage that had been intended for his butler. He demonstrated dazzling energy but a rare capacity to arouse suspicion. One historian described him as being 'mistrusted by an awesome array of the great and the good', and a biographer entitled an examination of his life *A Study in Failure*.

He was, of course, Winston Churchill. And he very nearly died that way: unfulfilled, under-appreciated and spread-eagled on the bonnet of a New York motor car on Fifth Avenue in 1931. He had not even made the name entirely his own. When news of his accident was broadcast on American radio, there was initially some confusion about whether the injured man was indeed the British politician or an undistinguished American novelist of the same name.

Churchill had set off from his hotel that night to find his friend Bernard Baruch's house without knowing the exact address. When his taxi driver couldn't help him, Churchill asked to walk the rest of the way, hoping that he would recognize the house once he was on foot. Instead, crossing Fifth Avenue from the Central Park side, he was run over by an unemployed mechanic called Mario Contasino.

Churchill just about remained conscious as he was rushed to Lenox Hill Hospital. He insisted that the accident was entirely his fault and even invited Contasino to visit him in hospital. When his bullishness gave way to reflection he admitted how easily the accident could have proved fatal. 'I do not understand why I was not broken like an eggshell,' he reflected, 'or squashed like a gooseberry.' He had deep wounds on his forehead and thighs, and suffered an attack of pleurisy in the hospital.

Determined not to alarm friends, Churchill ordered that no details of his ailments be given out. But his own telegrams, beneath the typically adventurous tone, suggest that he knew how close to death he had come. 'Pretty close,' he wrote to his son Randolph. Ever the opportunist, Churchill's next telegram was to the *Daily Mail*. He proposed 'two articles in quick succession ... upon how it feels to be run over by a motor car or some such title. Have complete recollection of whole event & believe can produce literary gem about 2,400 words'.

As part of his research for the article, Churchill telegraphed a scientist asking about the physical force of the crash. The professor replied: 'Collision equivalent falling thirty feet onto pavement, equal six thousand footpounds of energy. Equivalent stopping ten pound brick dropped six hundred feet, or two charges of buckshot pointblank range ... Congratulations on preparing suitable cushion, and skill in taking bump.'

Churchill's article earned him £600 (about £8,500 in today's money) at home and even more when it was syndicated around the world. He wrote to Randolph, 'I rather plume myself upon having had the force to conceive, write and market this article so soon after the crash. I received a great price for it, but find it very dearly bought.'

Churchill certainly retained his priorities in hospital. As it was the age of Prohibition, he managed to persuade his American doctor to write a note for him: 'This is to testify that the post-accident concussion of Hon. Winston S. Churchill necessitates the use of alcoholic spirits especially at meal times.'

But Clementine Churchill wasn't taken in by her husband's misleadingly jaunty tone. A month after the crash, she wrote how Churchill remained 'terribly depressed at the slowness of his recovery' from his 'terrible physical injury'. Lady

Lytton wrote to Churchill, crediting Clemmie's calming influence as central to his recovery. 'What a wonderful escape you had, my dear – sharp enough to make one's heart stop beating . . . What tremendous luck – Winston luck – that Clemmie was with you.'

III

Churchill thought his career might be drawing to a close, even before the car accident. He was about to publish *Thoughts and Adventures*, and the tone of the book implies that he believed his life to be somehow complete. The Preface describes the uncertainties 'through which a man of my generation, now in its twelfth lustre, has passed and is passing'.

In an extraordinary coincidence, one of the essays, 'A Second Choice', written just before his car accident in 1931, explicitly addresses the theme of luck. Churchill used a rhetorical construction – would we want to live our lives over again if we were given a 'second choice'? – to introduce his real theme of chance and fortune. Churchill begins by remembering a moment of apparently bad luck that turned out to have fortuitous consequences.

If, for instance, when I went to Monte Carlo and staked my money on red, as I usually do, having preference for the optimistic side of things, and the whirling ivory ball had fallen into a red slot in the roulette wheel instead of falling, as it nearly always did on these occasions, into a black slot, I might have made a lot of money ... On the other hand, if fired by my good luck I had continued to gamble, I might have become an habitué of the tables, and should now be one of those melancholy shadows we see creeping in the evening around the gaming and so-called pleasure resorts of Europe.

If winning at roulette can ruin your life, smoking can save it. Churchill reproaches himself for his addiction to nicotine – the money he has wasted on it and the damaging effect on his health. And yet in the trenches in the First World War, he had 'turned back to get that matchbox in Flanders', taking him out of the way of a 'shell which pitched so harmlessly a hundred yards ahead'. We can picture the glee on Churchill's face as he sat at his desk, lighting up another cigar, writing that smoking had, after all, been very good for his health.

Churchill credits luck for saving his life in an even earlier adventure, when he was captured during the Boer War in 1899. His armoured train was attacked and partially derailed by the Boers. But the engine remained on the tracks, and for two hours, despite heavy bombardment, Churchill bravely tried to get the engine moving again. He removed his own pistol from his side in his struggle to restart the engine. As a result, he was unarmed when he was confronted by a mounted Boer just twenty yards away. Had Churchill still been armed, he would not have surrendered, and so hugely increased his own chances of being killed.

After South Africa and Flanders, no wonder Churchill

thanked his luck: 'If we look back on our past life we shall see that one of its most usual experiences is that we have been saved by the consequences of our folly, and frustrated in our acts of wisdom and virtue, because of random interventions between cause and effect.'

In fact, Churchill's 'A Second Choice' underplays the role of good fortune in his surviving the Boer War. The full picture is even more extraordinary. At the battle of Spion Kop, a bullet cut through the feather of his hat, but the damage done was only sartorial.

Then there was his perilous escape from prison in Pretoria after his capture on the railway. Getting over the prison wall was one thing. But safety lay 280 miles away in Lourenço Marques in Portuguese East Africa. With nowhere to sleep at 1.30 a.m. on the second night after his escape, near the mining town of Witbank, Churchill had no alternative but to risk appealing to the kindness of strangers, gambling that he might be able to persuade or bribe them not to turn him in. He knocked at a door, only to find that it belonged to an English mine manager who quickly discovered his true identity and agreed to help him. Fortified with food, whisky and cigars, Churchill was lowered down a mine shaft, where he remained, safely out of harm's way, until the search for the escaped prisoner had calmed down.

The same tricks of chance applied to his political career. In 1923 Churchill lost his constituency election as a Liberal MP. An unlucky – it seemed – attack of appendicitis prevented him from his usual buoyant electioneering. 'In the twinkling of an eye I found myself without an office, without a seat, without a party, and without an appendix.'

Losing his seat, however, had its advantages. As he was no longer a Liberal MP, Churchill was spared any share of responsibility for the Liberals' unpopular decision to put the Labour Party into office. That allowed him – when he once again changed sides and returned to the Conservative Party in 1924 – to campaign as an enemy of socialism. In short, it took appendicitis to make him a Tory again – the party home from which he would eventually become Prime Minister.

Churchill had relied on remarkable luck in every sphere of his life, even before he unexpectedly leapfrogged Lord Halifax to become Prime Minister in 1940. We scarcely need to ask: what if a bullet had been an inch nearer the target; what if his pistol had stayed on his hip; what if a random door had belonged to a Boer not an Englishman; what if a box of matches hadn't been left behind; what if appendicitis hadn't cost him his seat; what if Contasino's car had been moving a fraction more quickly?

There would have been no Churchill to oppose appeasement in the 1930s, no Churchill to take over from Neville Chamberlain, no Churchill to galvanize Britain as it stood alone in 1940. What then? A successful German invasion . . . an occupied Nazi Britain . . . an isolationist America staying out of the war. If one unemployed mechanic had been driving a little faster, the man most commonly cited as the greatest of all Englishmen would have been remembered as a thwarted talent, and the whole history of the second half of the twentieth century would have been radically different.

IV

History is not always the beneficiary of slow driving. Earlier in 1931, a different pedestrian was knocked over during a car accident. On this occasion, however, the man's survival would have catastrophic consequences.

On 22 August 1931, John Scott-Ellis, a young Englishman who had just left Eton, was taking his new red Fiat for a spin around Munich. After an undistinguished career at Eton – he blamed 'ingrained laziness or lack of will' – Scott-Ellis's family encouraged him to spend some time in Germany so he could learn a new language.

After a week in his new city, on a clear, sunny day, Scott-Ellis bought his gleaming red Fiat and gave it a test drive around the streets of Munich. As he drove up Ludwigstrasse, he took a right turn into Briennerstrasse. But a pedestrian crossed the road without looking left – just as Churchill would do on Fifth Avenue four months later. 'He walked off the pavement, more or less straight into my car,' Scott-Ellis recalled.

After the crunch, the pedestrian was knocked down on one knee. Scott-Ellis was relieved to see him haul himself back onto his feet. Reassured that he hadn't seriously injured anyone, Scott-Ellis drove on – hoping the crash hadn't been witnessed by the Munich policeman who had been directing traffic.

Three years later, Scott-Ellis, now twenty-one, was sitting in a box waiting for the opera to begin at the Residenztheater.

In the adjacent box, he saw the same man he had knocked over. Having introduced himself, Scott-Ellis enquired whether the man remembered the incident. He did indeed. Nonetheless, Scott-Ellis recalled the man being 'quite charming to me for a few moments.' Their conversation was interrupted by the orchestra; the prelude had begun.

Scott-Ellis became a distinguished man. In 1946, he inherited the title Baron Howard de Walden and became one of the great British racehorse owners. He often told the story of that crash in Munich in 1931: 'For a few seconds, perhaps, I held the history of Europe in my rather clumsy hands. He was only shaken up, but had I killed him, it would have changed the history of the world.'

He had knocked over Adolf Hitler.

II

'Blessings'

'Never in the field of human conflict was so much owed by so many to so few.' Churchill's line captured the achievements of the Royal Air Force pilots who fought in the Battle of Britain. That summer of 1940 was the closest Britain came to falling to Nazi Germany. Defiance, resilience and endurance were Britain's greatest contribution to the fight against fascism.

The line was Churchill's finest hour, too. So much is conveyed, with such generosity of spirit, in so few words – the writer and the statesman in perfect sync. But not all of 'The Few' agree with him. I learnt a different version of events when I visited Bill Green, a spritely ninety-four, who flew Hurricanes in the Battle of Britain.

'I'm sure I originated the quotation: the Battle of Britain was not won by "The Few". It was won by a few of the few. That is an absolute fact. There were two sorts of pilots:

proper ones, and the rest. The first type had lots of experience. In 1937 the RAFVR invited volunteers who were qualified as pilots to go into regular service. Ginger Lacey, Paul Farnes and Hawkeye Lee (who would later become famous "aces") all did this. They were all earning a lot more in the Air Force than in their old jobs. They acquired hundreds of hours in the Hurricane or the Spitfire. So flying was second nature to them. They didn't have to think about it. It was these men, the experienced pilots, who did all the damage to the German planes. They could fly on instinct and focus on the fighting.'

Bill pauses for a moment for dramatic effect: 'Then there were the sprogs like me. We had little or no experience of flying. And we were shot out of the sky in short order. That's the way it was. We were all shot down or wounded. So the old sweats, the real pilots, had to carry on. They were tired, I can tell you. But they were the people who won the Battle of Britain.' At ninety-four, I suppose, you are long past wanting more credit than you deserve.

I'm sitting with Bill in his retirement home in Clevedon, under an hour's drive from Bristol. It's a small coastal town with ornamental gardens, a model railway and a pebbled shore, the sort of place where families like my father's liked to go for day trips.

Dad suffered the biggest trauma of his early life in Clevedon. In 1951, aged nine, he nearly drowned in the salt-water pool next to the beach. He had sunk to the bottom before a professional lifeguard fished him out – nearly dead, with water pouring from his nose and mouth. For us – the Smiths – Clevedon was a near wrong-turn in our family history. To be more accurate, had the road forked in the other direction, had my father not been pulled out, there would be no Smith family to have a history.

I can see that beach from Bill Green's living room, one of his two private rooms at the retirement hotel. It's hard to accept he is ninety-four. You could just about manufacture a photo to make him look his age – though it would require an unkind photographer. But in person, when you are sitting opposite him, watching him move snappily around the room smartly dressed in a short-sleeved khaki shirt and cravat, it just doesn't seem possible. It is partly the precision of his speech, the crispness of his manner, his impatience with fools and foolishness. But, above all, it is his impish, irreverent spirit that seems undimmed, unbowed. Ninety-four? It's hard to believe.

The fates once seemed determined to keep Bill Green from having a successful life. 'When I was eleven, at elementary school in Bristol, I was entered for a scholarship for the grammar school. The headmaster handed me an envelope and said, "Give this to your mother." So I took it home unopened. My mother opened it and read it through. It was a scholarship. She tore it up. "You don't want any of that rubbish. You'll have had plenty of education by the time you're fourteen."'

Another leg-up the social ladder had already been refused him. Bill's father was a night porter at the Grand Hotel in

Bristol. 'It was owned by Mrs Raymond. My father showed one guest his room and didn't like the look of him. Not long after, he heard screaming in the penthouse. The owner was being throttled by the guest. My father dragged him on to the landing, and knocked him out and he fell down the stairs, where he was arrested.

'My father died soon after of diabetes, a month before I was born. Mrs Raymond came to our house to thank us – she was sure my father had saved her life. "I would like to finance your boy going to a private school and right through university." My mother replied, "I'm sorry, but we never accept charity." Really, my mother didn't want to part with me.'

The what-ifs are irresistible. 'I've often pondered what might have happened if my mother had accepted it, or if I'd gone to the grammar school with my scholarship. Well, I wouldn't have met my wife for a start, so it was all planned to perfection.' The story captures the man: light, optimistic, precise, amused, matter of fact.

Deprived of a privileged education, Bill joined the Air Force aged nineteen as an aircraft fitter and engineer. The educated elite flew the planes; people like Bill serviced them. 'All the pilots then were commissioned officers. But I talked my way in. I was nothing if not audacious. I was the only engineer in the squadron who ended up flying. Others would have been better qualified and they would have been better at it. But they never asked. There is an old Arab proverb, "The baby that doesn't cry gets no milk."'

I had arranged to meet Bill because I'd been told his life had been marked by extraordinary encounters with luck. But it would be overstating the case to argue that his life was all determined by chance. His spirit and willpower played an undeniable part, too. His transition from mending planes to flying them was so fast and shambolic that he must have wondered what he had talked himself into. 'I'd been trained on World War One biplanes – no retractable undercarriage, no flaps, no oxygen, nothing. They were basic. I was halfway through training when I was sent to Hornchurch in August 1940. There I'd be able to train on a Master, a dual-controlled modern trainer, which was more like the Spitfire and the Hurricane.'

What was the training procedure for a novice pilot on an entirely new plane? 'They simply said, "Off you go!" So I flew it round north Kent and landed it. And he said, "Oh, you're fine, you don't need more training – you'd better get back to Biggin, it's getting dark."' I look for signs that Bill is exaggerating, telling tall tales from his glory days. Instead, I see the calm, clear-eyed expression of someone stating the facts.

Two days later, on 8 August, an officer asked him if he knew the Hurricane from his days as an engineer. 'He said, "Green, were you a tradesman before you were a pilot?" – my class must have been written in oil across my forehead – and I said, yes, I was. "Oh, then you know all about them. You see that one over there with a P on it. Go and sit in it and when you feel comfortable just take off."' Bill's training up to this point had consisted of half a training course on old

First World War planes, and one quick breeze around north Kent in a Master. Now he was being invited to climb into a Hurricane and simply take off, just like that? 'Absolutely. As God is my witness. I sat in the Hurricane for a while, then took off. Nearly frightened myself to death. This is the way it was. It was like going from a farm tractor to a Formula One Ferrari with no training.'

Bill built up a meagre total of six hours' flying time in a Hurricane, taking repaired aircraft to Biggin Hill, Northolt and Gravesend. 'On 19 August, I took one across to Gravesend late in the afternoon. I had the fortune – or *mis*fortune – to run into my Commanding Officer. He said, "Hello, Green, how many hours have you done?" I said six. He said, "They're too blankety-blank slow there. Get back to Biggin. We'll train you faster than that." I said, "When do you want me back?" Looking up at the darkening sky, he said, "Tonight!"

'So I went back to get my toothbrush. But what I didn't know is that the day before –18 August – my squadron had lost five aircraft and five pilots. Four planes had been shot down by Gerhard Schöpfel, the German ace. If it hadn't been for the fact that the fourth one blew up and covered his aircraft in black oil, and he couldn't see, and so had to get back to France, he would have shot the lot down. That's why the Commanding Officer wanted me back to fly a Hurricane.'

Speaking softly now, Bill adds, 'That's the way it was,' his catchphrase for the many things that were firmly out of his control. 'So I had a cup of cocoa and a cheese sandwich, and was given a bed next to Ginger Lacey – who became quite famous – and I got my head down and went to sleep. In the middle of the night, there was a light flashing in my face and someone shaking me, "Get up, get up." I said, "No, I've only just arrived, my name is Green." He said, "I know, you're Green." I found myself walking down to these Hurricanes with Ginger Lacey asking him what it was all about. We flew from Hawkinge because it was so close to France, only three or four minutes' flying time in a Hurricane. That was my first contact with the enemy, 20 August 1940. I'd assumed there would be a period of learning a bit about it. I had no idea.'

Bill's Battle of Britain followed the pattern of his theory of the few of the few. Sprogs like him didn't last long. On 29 August, nine days into his active flying career, he was hit flying over Deal. 'A hole appeared in my windscreen bang in front me, as big as my fist. Immediately, I started getting covered in engine coolant, glycol. I realized this aeroplane was finished and I had to get out. But I only got as far as putting the weight on to my feet, my bottom just off the seat, and bang, I found myself out in space, rolling forward, frantically trying to find the parachute ripcord. I thought, "I'll never find this ripcord." But I did and I pulled and thought, "Everything will be great now – it'll open up and I'll float down."'

But the parachute didn't open, even then. 'The cords on the drogue parachute were completely severed. So as soon as it activated, it just jetted off into space, and the main canopy on which I was sitting had nothing to drag it from its pack, so it just fell from its pack, and wrapped itself around me two or three times.

'I fully expected to die. What else, when you're falling from 20,000 feet? I'd only been married twelve weeks. I remember trying to seek my end with thoughts of her. I wasn't a Christian at the time. But I remember saying, "Please God, open this bloody parachute." It was an almost impossible situation, because my parachute was wrapped around me. Either I had to roll backwards to release the parachute, or the wind would somehow magically get under one of the folds. That's obviously what happened. The wind got under one of the folds and puffed it open. There was a jolt, I was kicked backwards, and I realized I was all right. The quietude that hit me then made more impact than any noise I've ever heard in my life.

'Would you like some coffee, Ed?' Bill asks, as though it were of equal importance. 'I was hit at 20,000 feet. A falling body falls at 205.3 feet per second – about 1,000 feet in five seconds. I was falling for one minute twenty seconds.' The engineer in him is delighted to get into the physics. 'When the parachute opened I was about 250 feet from the ground. That's only a few seconds, if I'd kept free-falling. I looked to my right, and the pylon cables were level with me. And I looked to my left and the trees were above me. I landed at Mill Hill farm, near the east Kent village of Elham. A couple of blokes came running from a farmhouse with shotguns but they realized I was English. When I tried to get up, I fell down again. I'd been hit in the right leg and didn't even realize it. That was the end of the Battle of Britain for me.'

But it wasn't the end of Bill's war. His fall was only one of a series of freakily close encounters with death. Having convalesced he resumed his duties at Exeter airfield. One day, he was responsible for organizing the flare path, the paraffin cans that lined the runway. He was driving up the runway in a truck to deposit the paraffin cans, each accompanied by an airman. 'I saw three Heinkel 111s [German bombers] flying straight up the runway. All hell let loose. I remember thinking, "What am I going to do?" For some reason – I don't know why – I turned at right angles.'

It was a random decision that saved his life. 'The bomb went off just where I'd been. There was a huge blue flash and a noise. If you can imagine a whip crack multiplied by a million – that was what it was like. My truck went up in the air, but returned to land, and I managed to get it across the perimeter track and rolled into the ditch.'

When Bill got the truck moving again, he drove over to look at the damage. When he reached the last of the eight airmen who were positioned to the side of the runway, Bill heard a voice of disbelief. 'Gosh, Sarge, I never expected to see you again,' the airman told him. 'There was a huge blue flash right where your truck was.' There was a crater in the middle of the runway, sixty feet by thirty feet. If he'd driven straight on, the bomb would have landed right on top of him.

'I'll never know what made me turn the truck one way and not the other. You'd have to say that was one of my luckiest moments.'

In 1941, Bill was trained as a flying instructor. 'It was a safe, cushy job with nobody shooting at you. Not many people gave up being an instructor. But I had a guilt complex that I'd been shot out of the Battle of Britain without really being given a fair crack of the whip. I had a young son at the time. I couldn't have a situation where he asked me about the war, and I simply told him my bit about the Battle of Britain. So I had to get back to operational flying.

'I eventually managed it. By 1944, I'd been posted to 56th Squadron who had just converted from Typhoons to Tempest Vs – very fast, modern fighters, the last of the piston-movement fighters we produced before the Meteor jet. It did 420mph, twenty-four cylinders,' he adds, full of awe at the mechanical virtuosity.

'After the invasion of Holland, we were flying out of a place between Eindhoven and Nijmegen. I was doing fine with the Tempest Vs. Until 22 February 1945 when I was hit in my port wing by an American Mustang, six holes about inch and half in diameter down six feet from where I was sitting. There was a blue flame burning in each of the holes like a Bunsen burner. So I kicked on the rudder bar to carry any flames away from the fuselage, and flew the plane down to about 400 feet. I wanted to get the plane across the battle line rather than become a PoW.

'I thought I'd got away with it. And suddenly I felt the heat of the flames sear my face and I realized I had to get out of the aeroplane. The technique was to pull the pin of the Sutton harness that strapped you in the aeroplane and pull the red knob on the instrument-panel to jettison the hood at the same time, while simultaneously kicking the stick forward with your foot. All you hope is that you don't hit the tail of the plane as you float out of it. Sometimes people died hitting their heads on the tail. But it was better than dying in a burning aeroplane. I shot out into space at 400 feet, and the first thing I remember seeing was the parachute pack floating out there, on the end of the straps. And I thought "God, not again. I've only got 400 feet this time!" So I yanked the cord anyway and bingo I was okay.

'I was found by a German farmer. I shot my hands up. He said "Are you armed?" And I said no. He said, "Put down your hands, I speak English better than you. I was educated at Cincinnati University in the USA. Now you must pick up your parachute and go."

'"Do you mean 'come' or 'go'?" I said.

'"I meant 'come'," he replied.

'"Well your English needs polishing, for a start. There's a big difference between coming and going as far as I'm concerned."'

As a prisoner of war, Bill was taken first to an airfield lock-up, then to an interrogation centre in Oberhausen, then finally to a PoW camp in Nuremberg. Only later, after the war had finished, did he discover how close he had come to being in the wrong place at the wrong time.

'I came out of the service in November 1945, and we moved to the Midlands. But my mother-in-law phoned from Bristol to say there was a letter in the *Bristol Evening Post* enquiring whether anyone knew where I was. It was the German farmer who'd taken me prisoner trying to find out if I was alive. So I got the address and wrote to him. I got a letter back explaining why he had written. His letter explained that a renegade German soldier, "a boisterous Nazi and a ruffian", had murdered all the British PoWs in the airfield lock-up where I had been taken after being captured.'

The German farmer was distraught that he might have inadvertently delivered Bill into the hands of a lunatic murderer. 'In fact, the murder happened three days after I'd been moved on. So that was a near do, wasn't it? If he'd decided to do what he did three days before it would have been me.'

How does he account for all that luck – the wind blowing open the parachute one second before he died, avoiding the bomb on the flare path, the near-miss at the lock-up? Bill has a more uneasy relationship with the concept of luck. 'As a Christian, I don't call it luck. I call them blessings.' It is one of the few times he mentions his faith. But it would be dishonest of me not to mention the distinction he draws between my secular concept of luck and his religious belief.

It is, however, a distinction rather than a dichotomy. Bill Green perfectly embodies the idea that believing in luck – or blessings – should make us humble. Perhaps the earlier chapter about my American friend Andrew, an atheist interviewed by an agnostic, stacked the deck too far. My sister, who is a Catholic, complained to me after reading it: 'The conclusions you draw from thinking about luck are familiar to anyone who thinks about God.' If your faith is like Bill Green's – a faith that keeps him joyous and humble, spirited and audacious yet also conscious of his vulnerability – then maybe my sister is right.

After a tussle over the lunch bill – 'I'll be very, very cross if you pay for this,' he said sternly – Bill walks me to my car, parked by Clevedon beach. He had spoken almost uninterrupted for four hours, never once repeating himself or losing his thread. He wanted to set me straight on one last thing. 'I've really enjoyed chatting. But I am very mindful of the fact that I am no hero.'

Anyone can come close to dying several times, as Bill did. Very few take such full advantage – in terms of the joy they experience and the contribution they make. Bill Green, in every respect, is one of the very few.

12

Accidents II

I

But wasn't Churchill – let alone Bill Green – atypical? Someone who is a soldier, gambler, bon viveur, journalist, author and adventurer before becoming Prime Minister obviously has an unusual degree of exposure to life-changing strokes of luck. Surely other careers are less dependent on blind luck?

I am not so sure. Consider Margaret Thatcher. In the mid-1970s, Keith Joseph, as the ideological champion of the right, was widely tipped to become the next leader of the Conservative Party. But a disastrous speech spiked Joseph's career before he had the chance to push for the top. He had long allowed Alfred Sherman to write his speeches, and they were so good that he gave up looking over them carefully before he read them out. So Joseph went to speak in Birmingham in 1974 with an unread speech in his pocket. He then discovered that Sherman had written a speech saying that the trouble was that the proletariat, especially 'those of low intelligence', were having too many children. So the choice was to give them contraception or face national 'degeneration'. Joseph was then brutally pilloried in *Private Eye* as 'Sir Sheath'. After the speech, his career was in tatters.

The historian Norman Stone recalls the crucial scene between Joseph and Thatcher: 'They met that evening in Flood Street, where Mrs T was cooking – fried eggs or something in the kitchen – and Keith Joseph said with his head in his hands, "Well, I can't possibly stand after this," as the wolves bayed outside. She came dancing in with her frying pan and said, "Well, if you're not going to stand, I will."' Consider the impact of one unchecked speech on the course of political history: on the Cold War, the miners' strike, the Falklands War and Britain's special relationship with Reagan's America.

We have already referred to Napoleon's line about lucky generals. Less well known is how much his own life demonstrates the power of luck and accident. As a very young man, Napoleon sought service with the greatest fighting force of the age (Britain's) and applied to the Admiralty in London. His approach was ignored. What if it had been accepted? There would be no 'Trafalgar' Square or 'Waterloo' station. But Europe would have been spared several wars and thousands of death. The then Lords of the Admiralty have a lot to answer for.

II

Did a sandwich start the First World War? Or should blame be attributed to a Pljeskavica, a meat patty popular in the Balkans?

Most people know about the 'shot that started the First World War', the assassination of archduke Franz Ferdinand by Gavrilo Princip on 28 June 1914. Less well known are the circumstances that led to it.

Princip was one of seven assassins, a group of Bosnian-born Serbs who wanted to promote the cause of a greater Serbia by killing the heir to the Austro-Hungarian throne. They decided that Ferdinand's visit to Sarajevo was the ideal opportunity.

The seven assassins positioned themselves strategically at different points on the archduke's procession through Sarajevo. The first attempt on Ferdinand's life was made by Nedelijo Cabrinovic, who threw a grenade at the open-topped car carrying the archduke. But the grenade was old and bounced off the limousine before exploding under the next vehicle, injuring several officers, but leaving Ferdinand unhurt.

Cabrinovic tried unsuccessfully to commit suicide by swallowing cyanide (it was too old) and jumping into a river (it was only four inches deep). Meanwhile, the failed bombing seemed to have ruined the chances of the other would-be assassins. The motorcade was cancelled and the Archduke hurried off to the town hall, presumably to safety.

Disconsolate that their moment had gone, the conspirators dispersed, including Gavrilo Princip, who decided on a visit to Moritz Schiller's delicatessen. What better way could there be to get over the disappointment of a failed assassination than a light snack?

But the archduke's chaffeur took a wrong turn as he left the town hall, mistakenly turning into Franz Joseph street, directly in front of Schiller's deli. Princip, having given up on killing Ferdinand, is now just a few feet away from his target. Princip fires two shots. The first kills Ferdinand's wife, the second kills the archduke himself. Fatally for Europe, the assassination triggers the descent into war between the Entente Powers (Britain, France and Russia) and the Central Powers (Germany and Austria-Hungary).

Historians still debate whether Princip's sandwich was left half eaten on the table. Some argue that a Sarajevo café was much more likely to have served him a Pljeskavica. Others maintain that it was too early for lunch, and the lack of evidence that Princip placed an order at the deli.

A deeper criticism holds that an isolated event such as Ferdinand's assassination cannot possibly explain an event as complex and calamitous as the First World War. In this version of history, the assassination merely lit the fuse, but the tinderbox would surely have exploded anyway.

Perhaps. But had Princip *not* killed Ferdinand in Sarajevo, the outbreak of the First World War would have at the very least been delayed. A war delayed is a war averted. Had the Entente Powers and the Central Powers not gone to war in

August 1914, a future war, even if had happened, would have followed a different course.

The First World War as we know it – in all its horror and with its deep and disastrous consequences – was indeed triggered by a wrong turn by a chauffeur and an interrupted visit to a delicatessen.

III

Can the destiny of an entire country be determined by luck? We don't need to go as far back as Napoleon to think of a perfect example.

Look at the diverging experiences of European countries today. Many face a bleak immediate future. Britain's crippling national debt has led to deep cuts in every department except the NHS and overseas aid. France's budget deficit in 2010 was €144 billion. Elsewhere, it's even worse. The public finances in Greece and Ireland were so disastrous that they have required international bailouts.

Almost every European country is addressing a deeply uncomfortable truth: that, following the economic crisis, it has to cut the benefits previously conferred on its citizens. Lollipop ladies are being laid off, public libraries boarded up, forests put up for sale, Accident and Emergency wards closed. Welcome to Europe in the early 2010s.

Except in Norway, that is. While everyone else is in debt, Norway is sitting on a surplus. Such riches continue to fund the expansion of the welfare state. According to the IMF, Norway has the fourth highest GDP per capita in the world, behind only Qatar, Luxembourg and Singapore. But that doesn't quite capture the pleasures of being Norwegian. The UN has devised a Human Development Index (HDI) – calculated from data on life expectancy and education, as well as wealth. In 2010, Norway led the world in HDI.

And while its European neighbours fret about their exposure to the next crisis, Norway can sit on its financial cushion and happily gaze over its fjords with the satisfaction of a man with deep pockets in a time of austerity. So what makes Norway so clever?

It was a different story in the 1960s. Yes, Norway was still relatively affluent. But its growth trailed behind that of its Scandinavian neighbour Sweden, let alone the world's economic titans. Norway was a beautiful country but an industrial backwater. The thought of envying Norway – from an economic perspective – would never have occurred to the British or Americans.

What was it that turned the tables?

In October 1962, Phillips Petroleum sent in an application to search for oil in Norwegian territory in the North Sea. Other companies were also looking for oil, but this 'race' was characterized by mild interest rather than urgent dedication.

Phillips's enthusiasm was not helped by dismal results. The first well was drilled in the summer of 1966, but it was dry.

The pattern of failure was the same for the next three years: in total, thirty-two wells were drilled in the North Sea, and none of them was commercially viable. Worse still, this kind of exploration was proving to be more expensive and more difficult than anything in Phillips's history.

By the winter of 1969, the mission was becoming dangerous as well as fruitless. One evening, the drilling rig nearly capsized and an emergency evacuation took place. Facing spiralling costs, no returns and dwindling hope, finally, a stark message was sent to Norway from Phillips's headquarters in Bartlesville, Oklahoma: 'Do not drill any more wells.'

Only misfortune – or so it seemed – kept them out at sea. Phillips had prepaid for the use of a rig, the *Ocean Viking*, and were unable to sub-lease it to anyone else. So Phillips was forced to carry on paying daily charges for *Ocean Viking*, whether it was drilling or not. Forced to stay on – against their better judgement – they decided to make one last effort to find some oil. In November 1969, going through the motions of exploration, long after they had been advised from above to stop digging, the *Ocean Viking* struck oil 10,000 feet below the seabed.

In terms of technical difficulty, it was practically a miracle. It was just after the American astronauts had landed on the moon, and the *Ocean Viking* superintendent, as he looked at the golden sheen of the oil, compared the achievements: 'What the astronauts have done is great, but how about this?' The North Sea, in an instant, had become a hotspot for the world's oil industry. At first, there were dreams of an oil field that might last for a decade, perhaps two. But Ekofisk, as the oil well became known, was far, far bigger than that. It was the last time for decades that a rig such as *Ocean Viking* would struggle to find employment in the North Sea.

Months later, at a meeting in London, a senior executive was asked about the methods used by Phillips to diagnose the oil field. 'Luck,' he replied.

Ekofisk was the biggest Christmas present in Norwegian history. Over the next forty years, 3,000 wells were drilled in the Norwegian continental shelf. And the oil is not drying up any time soon. All mineral wealth is finite, of course, but Ekofisk is predicted to last until 2050. A single chance discovery turned into the most transformational event in the entire development of Norway's modern economy. Gross income from the Norwegian petroleum sector has now generated 8,000 billion kroner, and a third of that has been siphoned into the bank. In 2010, Norway had a trade surplus of 341.5 billion kroner (£37 billion).

Perhaps Norway was culturally predisposed to make the most of its good luck. The Norwegians retain a great fondness for a mythic folk hero, Askeladden (or Ash Lad). In the folk tales of Peter Christen Asbjørnsen and Jørgen Moe, Askeladden owes his mythic triumphs to chance as often as skill. He is the younger brother, the chancer, the one who seems to have no luck but finds his luck in the end.

Norway, too, had to wait for its good luck. It achieved independence from Sweden only in 1905. And for much of its history, it has lived in the shadow of its more prosperous neighbour. When fortune turned, Norway was determined not to waste it. It has a Government Pension Fund that tucks away a good portion of the country's oil revenues for long-term investments. It is worth almost £500 billion, the largest pension fund in Europe, designed to prepare Norway for a time when North Sea oil runs out. There is an old Norwegian proverb: 'Luck is loaned, not owned.'

However skilfully it has played its hand, Norway was certainly dealt the aces. It was Ekofisk that gave it the opportunity to become Europe's 'outlier' and anomaly. If the Phillips Petroleum legal team had been able to offload *Ocean Viking*, if the orders from above had been followed through, then Norway's hospitals, schools and public finances would be in the same perilous state as everywhere else.

And I wouldn't have spent today looking into opening a savings account in Norwegian kroner – just in case both the euro and sterling nosedive. As the Phillips executive cheerfully admitted, it was all down to that four-letter word . . .

IV

It's hard to stop, once you start thinking about the power of accidents. What looks like wisdom turns out to be luck.

There is a popular view that England's triumph in the 2010–11 Ashes was the direct consequence of a long-term strategic plan. After the 5–0 trouncing in 2006–7, the argument runs, England commissioned the Schofield report, went back to the drawing board and devised a cunning plan which they ruthlessly executed over the next four years, culminating in Andrew Strauss lifting the Ashes urn at Sydney in January 2011.

According to this received version, the victory of 2010–11 was a coolly logical affair. Sure, the famous England win in 2005 might have relied a bit on luck, when Australian fast bowler Glenn McGrath, England's nemesis, twisted his ankle just before the second Test match. Not this time, though, surely? Except for one disaster in Perth, England were significantly better than Australia throughout 2010–11. Can't we all agree it was a scientific exercise in strategic foresight?

I hate to be a killjoy. And I am the first person to acknowledge how well England prepared and trained. But I'm not sure this elegant strategic theory holds up to even a splash of historical analysis. In 2008 – *after* the strategic review of English cricket – it was England's strategy to make Kevin Pietersen captain and Peter Moores coach. It surely cannot have been anyone's plan to watch their relationship fissure and then self-destruct so spectacularly in 2009?

If we want an honest history of the 2011 Ashes, we cannot ignore a trio of vital accidents, a chain of events that leads from Duncan Fletcher's eccentric judgement, to Kevin Pietersen's outspokenness, and finally to Michael Vaughan's dicky knee.

Take the captaincy, a central factor in any success story. In fact, Andrew Strauss may be the most pivotal leader in the modern history of English cricket.

Presumably, his suitability for the top job was never doubted by the selectors? Far from it. Strauss was not the selectors' first choice to captain his contemporaries. He was not even their second choice. He was made captain only when he was effectively the last man standing. Finding Strauss by such a circuitous route may have been absurd. But it is undeniably what happened.

Consider the outline of his path to the captaincy. It took England an awfully long time to get round to Strauss. When Michael Vaughan was injured in 2006, the captaincy shifted to Andrew Flintoff. It was only when Flintoff himself got injured that Strauss was handed the captaincy in the 2006 series against Pakistan. Strauss's response was a 3–0 series win and the best batting of his career. And yet Duncan Fletcher, the coach at the time, reverted to Flintoff for the disastrous 2006–7 Ashes tour. Many elements of that decision were odd. Fletcher's view that neither Flintoff nor Strauss had much captaincy experience failed to acknowledge Strauss's record at Middlesex. Fletcher said to Strauss before the 5–0 thrashing: 'You'll thank me for this one day.' That day has come now. It is unlikely that even Strauss's diplomatic skills could have rescued that calamitous tour. Strauss may indeed have been tainted by failure and discarded for the future. But what a tortuous, if not perverse, way for Fletcher to be proved right.

Strauss would be passed over again, in favour of Pietersen in 2008. The dominant reason was 'uniting the captaincy'. Where Pietersen was an automatic pick for all three forms of the game, Strauss was out of the one-day side at the time. The idea that the benefits of having an experienced captain could outweigh the perceived disadvantage of 'having' to pick Strauss in one-day cricket was laughed at as anachronistic. Pundits ridiculed the idea that a captain might force his way into the team through his leadership skills.

It was only Pietersen's direct personality that opened the door for Strauss's subtler gifts. Pietersen had initially taken to the captaincy – relishing his early press conferences and scoring a masterful hundred in his first innings. But within five months, having struggled to agree a working relationship with the coach, he seemed unprepared to carry on as captain with Moores and his support staff. It was widely reported, and nowhere denied, that Pietersen wanted wholesale changes or else he would consider his position as captain. The impasse became a public spat while Pietersen was away on safari and his stance was generally interpreted, not least by his employers, as an ultimatum. Ultimately, both Pietersen and Moores lost their jobs. It was a strange end to Pietersen's captaincy: he'd been appointed for his directness and hitherto unshakeable self-belief, qualities that duly brought about his sacking. In effect, Pietersen was appointed for being himself and then lost his job for being himself.

It was only at this point – with Flintoff injured, Vaughan retired and Pietersen demoted – the selectors looked for another man in his early thirties to captain England. There was only one candidate, Andrew Strauss. It is here that we see the strategic nature of the long-term plan: leave yourself with no other options.

It now seems obvious, with the benefit of hindsight, that Strauss had to captain England, and very likely that he would succeed once he did. But if we study the odds when the crucial moments occurred, we will see how improbable his journey has been. Did anyone think it was likely – when Flintoff and then Pietersen were made captain – that Strauss would captain England to Ashes victory in 2011? If so, they kept very quiet about it.

That Strauss eventually arrived owes much to his quiet resilience and mental strength. Where more conspicuously ambitious men fell by the wayside, victims of impatience, Strauss bided his time. Able but not intimidating, assured but not overbearing, analytical but not fretful, amenable but not supine, Strauss is a master of moderation. He is at ease in most company, from the dressing room to the boardroom. His greatest political talent is not appearing to be overly political. He never cared about walking into a room like a natural-born leader. Impressing people has never been important to him; what matters to Strauss is getting things done.

We cannot, however, tell the whole story through the personality of Strauss, as most profiles of him tend to do. Strauss was always unflappable, always resilient and always shrewd. They are unchanging strands of his character.

But they were clearly, on their own, insufficient to make him England captain. For that, he depended on a series of accidents: the blunders of coaches, and the outspokenness and injuries of his predecessors.

V

I was an exact contemporary of Strauss, and played against him many times at school and university. When I first met him, at an England Schools trial, he was not the kid in the county tracksuit earmarked for professional greatness. He just clipped the ball deftly off the back foot, a rare skill for a schoolboy, and let others brag about county contracts and bat deals. His apparent cricketing diffidence continued at university; he was always looking as though he should get more runs than he did. It was as though he had not yet been driven to access the ruthless strand of his character. Even in his early twenties, he was rarely singled out, unlike his prodigiously gifted Middlesex team-mate Owais Shah, as destined for greatness. Strauss slipped into the England team underneath everyone's radar, without fanfare or excessive expectations.

I got to know Strauss much better when I left Kent and joined him at Middlesex in 2005. He was enjoying a phenomenal start to his England career: after a hundred on debut in 2004, he scored more calendar runs in his first year as a Test cricketer than anyone in history, and, now in 2005, he belonged to an England team with a serious prospect of beating Australia for the first time in two decades. In short, he had a lot to feel good about.

The first time we shared a long car journey, on the way to play against Gloucestershire at Bristol, Strauss brought up the subject of luck. He listed the chance interventions that had helped him to score a hundred on debut the previous summer: 'Lord's was great to bat on, and New Zealand lacked Shane Bond [their injured star bowler]. Home ground, flat wicket, and you're off: so much of it is complete luck.'

It adds up to quite an unlikely sequence of probabilities. First, Michael Vaughan, then the England captain, twisted his knee and collapsed in the nets, so an extra batter needed to be called up. At the time, Vaughan was central to the England team – one of the best players in the world and a successful captain. No one could have guessed that an injury to Vaughan could have beneficial long-term consequences for English cricket. But it did – by providing the opportunity for Strauss to make his Test debut. Initially, it was thought that Mark Butcher would move from number three to opener, allowing Paul Collingwood to fill the vacancy in the middle order. But Butcher wanted to stay at three, so Collingwood was not selected, and Strauss was called into the team to open the batting. Strauss took the chance with both hands, becoming the first Englishman for eleven years to score a hundred on debut.

There would be one final intervention by chance. In the nervous 90s, when batsmen often get out in over-eager anticipation of reaching a hundred, Strauss hit the ball on to his stumps. But the ball didn't dislodge the bails, as it would 999 times out of a 1,000, and instead deflected for four runs. It was his day. It seemed that nothing would stop him.

He may well have needed all those runs. The England

management at the time were strongly committed to their core group of players. So even a good debut by Strauss would not have guaranteed his reselection. When Vaughan returned from injury, Strauss would have had to make way. Instead, his hundred led the experienced Nasser Hussain to choose to retire rather than stand in Strauss's way.

It was typically gracious and understated of Strauss to acknowledge the role of chance in the story. But almost every cricketer can tell a similar story, even if they are reluctant to admit it. When I recently asked Kevin Pietersen if he believed in luck, he paused thoughtfully, as though grappling with an uncomfortable idea. He and I were on the England 'A' tour to India in 2004, the first time he wore a shirt bearing the three lions of England. I had never played with anyone with such an epic degree of self-belief. His batting – his whole life – seemed to be driven by a deep sense of destiny. He projected the confidence of a man assured of greatness, unafraid of making enemies, determined to stamp his name in the record books. We had very different styles as players and as people, but I admired that frankness and reluctance to compromise.

So it was a mischievous question, to ask him about luck. I knew it ran slightly counter to his instincts. But when Pietersen focuses on something seriously, he rarely avoids saying what he believes to be true. 'Luck? Yeah, there's gotta be. Luck has to be huge. That dropped catch. I mean, how huge was that?' He is referring to the innings that defined his career. In the deciding match of the 2005 Ashes – the greatest, most fluctuating series of modern times – Pietersen found himself suddenly under pressure. His form had dipped and his critics were circling. Was this super-confident South African really the superstar he clearly yearned to be? 'If Warney had caught it, how differently would my life have turned out? I was under pressure. I hadn't scored a hundred all Ashes series. Who knows what would have happened ...' He trailed off, leaving the sentence unfinished.

But we know what *might* have happened. He might have been dropped. He might have fallen out of favour. He might have drifted out of the international scene. It sounds improbable now, given everything we know about him today – his 6,000 Test match runs and seventeen hundreds. But back then, when Warne dropped him on 13 at the Oval in September 2005, the shape of his career was not yet clear. He was still waiting for his first hundred.

He didn't have to wait long. He scored 158 that day, one of the great Ashes innings, helping England to win their first series against Australia since 1987. On the biggest day of his life, Pietersen played the role he felt he had been born to play. I always thought he was too good not to make it. But if Warne had held on to that catch, I might have been proved wrong. As Pietersen himself put it: 'Once things have happened, they seem inevitable. But they aren't at the time, are they?' Even in his story – one driven by his sense of destiny, and defined by vast ability and self-belief – there is still luck, always luck.

But a sample of one or two people is scarcely scientific.

That is an argument often made against using luck to explain events: it is too hard to measure. We'll never be able to peer into the inner workings of fortune, the argument runs. So let's discount luck and focus on giving credit where credit is due. But it's not always true. We can sometimes quantify luck, and sport is an especially useful tool. Where a normal career is difficult to measure, sports careers, especially in games such as cricket and baseball, can easily be broken down into bite-sized numerical chunks.

So two economists at the International Monetary Fund decided to use cricket careers to test a hypothesis: does luck matter more than we care to admit in deciding who succeeds at cricket and, by implication, elsewhere in life? It sounds improbable that the IMF is interested in cricket averages. But they were on to something.

They asked if there is an advantage in making your international debut in your home country as opposed to abroad. The authors took advantage of a pre-existing data set by analysing 790 cricketers from seven countries who made their international debuts between 1950 and 1985. What did they find? Unsurprisingly, specialist batters who made their debuts at home did better than those debuting abroad. It is self-evident that home advantage is stronger in cricket than in most sports because cricket is unusually bound up with the natural environment. The soil, the humidity, the temperature: each radically influences the nature of the contest. Being used to the conditions provides a clear advantage.

But the margin by which home debutants did better is astonishing. Specialist batsmen debuting at home score on average 32 per cent more than those debuting abroad. Let's put it in context. Thirty-two per cent is the difference between a good player and a great one. Sachin Tendulkar averages 56 over his career, 32 per cent more than Nasser Hussain's average of 37. Put differently, home debutants outperform away debutants by the same margin as Tendulkar outperformed Hussain. The researchers call home-debut players 'lucky' and abroad debut players 'unlucky'.

Secondly, the IMF study showed home-debut players then disproportionately got invited back for more Test matches. The reason is that national selectors fail to distinguish between 'lucky' and 'unlucky' debutants. In the language of economists, they do not 'control' for luck.

The third IMF finding is the most suggestive of all. There is a strong correlation between debut scores and career averages. Why? Having got off to a good start, players are more likely to benefit from batting in their right position. They also immediately establish confidence that they belong at that level. Added job security and enhanced self-belief become reinforcing advantages. In short, the luck of debuting at home endures throughout a player's career. It is not, of course, a guarantee of continued success. But it is a substantial leg-up on the ladder.

What is really being analysed here? It is not the luck of being picked in the first place. We are looking at how good luck increases your chances of *staying* picked. To return to the example of Strauss: the IMF paper addressed the luck of him debuting at Lord's, not the luck of Michael Vaughan's knee. The IMF report argues that a successful debut is like a good initial job placement. Consider the implications for the rest of life. What is the likelihood that normal employers will be able to distinguish between lucky and unlucky candidates?

The logic of the IMF study suggests they will not. After all, few jobs are chosen as scientifically or disinterestedly as cricket teams. Your dad can't slip your CV into the selectors' briefcase; a beautiful player can't charm his or her way through an interview. A selection panel that picked teams according to nepotism or on the basis of good looks would be unlikely to survive the attentions of the media or the demands of the fans. So while selectors may not be perfect, they're usually honest. It is in a selection panel's overwhelming self-interest to get their selections right. And yet they consistently fail to account for the luck experienced by rival players early in their careers.

If selection panels fail to shoot straight, normal employers – who have less incentive to get the decision right and usually less data at their disposal – must miss the target by an even greater distance. Most employment decisions are not made with the benefit of any transparent and quantitative data. That raises the question: how many stellar non-sporting careers were launched on the back of a similar lucky break?

Nor does luck 'even out', as the adage holds. An early lucky break stays lucky throughout your life. Once you're in a good job, advantages accumulate: you are surrounded by better colleagues, an enhanced network and greater challenges.

Chance events are not like weights, balanced in a scale, with good luck on one side and bad luck on the other. Instead, the intervention of luck is like a boulder that diverts the course of a stream: the course is changed — and stays changed for ever, whatever happens downstream. By then, it is a different life that is being altered. Luck not only intervenes; it persists.

13

It's the uncertainty, stupid

Is life a game of chess, where the player has a choice at every move, where skill and foresight can bring him success? Or is it rather backgammon, where a modicum of skill may speed or delay the result, but where the final outcome is determined by the repeated throw of the dice, which some might call blind chance and others the predetermined decision of God?

Bernard Lewis, *The Middle East*

I

It's not terribly cool, but another thing I did when I was injured was to take up backgammon. There are lots of things I like about backgammon: the aesthetic appeal of the board, the sound of the dice and the retro feel of the game.

But there were, I think, deeper reasons for being drawn to the game. With many backgammon moves, the dice do the thinking for me. Sometimes, of course the various options present a challenging decision. But often choice is limited because there is obviously a right decision that has been determined by the way the dice landed. There is certainly an element of skill, but you devolve the greater part of the game to luck. The dice drive the game; you are in a subordinate role. In that sense, backgammon is the opposite of chess, where the range of options is vastly more sophisticated and the role of chance negligible.

Fifteen years ago I would have laughed at the idea that I would ever derive much pleasure from a game where the result was heavily influenced by the random throw of the dice. But now, handing over such a degree of control to pure chance suits me perfectly. Why? Because I usually play backgammon after dinner, winding down after work. I have made enough difficult decisions for one day and I'm mostly happy for chance to make the remaining ones on my behalf. Backgammon fits the bill: you can enjoy a measure of competition and fun without having to think too much.

The chanciness of backgammon has two further advantages. First, when you lose, there is a ready-made excuse: you blame bad luck. In fact, it's more flexible than just an excuse, as you can adjust the theory to fit both victory and defeat. When I win, I credit skill; when I lose, I blame luck. I find it's a very good construction for a happy evening. For the very low blow, you can go one further and push your luck by saying to your opponent, 'Amazing I won that one since you had all the doubles.' Chance is an endless source of mischievous debate.

There is a connected reason why backgammon suited me. I took up the game for the first time aged thirty, but my opponent (my girlfriend) had played since childhood. So she was far better than I was. But backgammon's inherent luck element precluded me from suffering a relentless sequence of defeats. Through the sheer dumb luck of throwing better dice, I would occasionally beat a much better player. I still lost most of the time, but not so often that I gave up hope completely. Backgammon's large element of luck, I can see now, gave the underdog enough of a chance to stay interested.

That led me to a more serious question about other sports, a question I'd never considered before: do most sports fans prefer chess-type sports (where chance is negligible), or backgammon-type games (where chance is very important)? I'd always assumed that the human preference for narrative justice leads us to prefer games with the smallest possible degree of luck. But playing backgammon made me question the assumption that we want sport to be fair in the sense that the result is determined by ability rather than luck. If backgammon had been more just, it would have been boring for my girlfriend and me, given the unequal skills of the two players. Every game would have ended the same way, with me losing. (That's what would have happened if we'd been playing chess.)

The question is universal. What skill:luck ratio gives us the most satisfying mixture of justice (so the best team *usually* wins) and yet also sufficient narrative uncertainty (so the best team doesn't win *all* the time)? Put differently, what is the optimal degree of 'luckiness' in a sport?

And is it possible, weird as it sounds, that some sports could do with an injection of luck and a reduction of justice?

II

Anyone who knows Woody Allen's films will have noticed his obsession with luck. *Whatever Works*, for example, ends with one of Allen's typical meditations on the forces beyond our control: 'Don't kid yourself, it's by no means all up to your own human ingenuity. A bigger part of your existence is luck than you'd like to admit. Christ, you know the odds of your father's one sperm from the billions, finding the single egg that made you? Don't think about it, you'll have a panic attack.' It's a theme he returns to again and again, most memorably in *Match Point*, which opens with a scene at the exclusive London sports club, Queen's. The film opens with a tennis ball balancing on top of the net cord (the piece of wire that holds up the net) about to topple back on to one side of the net or the other. From the players' perspective, the time for skill and effort was all over. It was down to pure chance. Sport, Allen suggests, is just like life:

> The man who said 'I'd rather be lucky than good' saw deeply into life. People are afraid to face how great a part of life is dependent on luck. It's scary to think so much is out of one's

control. There are moments in a match when the ball hits the top of the net, and for a split second, it can either go forward or fall back. With a little luck, it goes forward, and you win. Or maybe it doesn't, and you lose.

I agree with the sentiment, but the details are technically wrong. To win a match in tennis you must win by two clear points; a margin of one point is never sufficient. So there is never a time when a ball balancing on the net could determine a match point that applied simultaneously to both players.

It's not just logic-chopping. There is a deeper objection to choosing tennis to illustrate the role of luck in sport. Tennis, like all sports, undoubtedly has *moments* that are dominated by luck. There are umpiring mistakes and moments when the ball balances on top of the net. But how often do those moments of luck prove critical, how often are tennis *results* really determined by luck?

Before the remarkable ascent of Novak Djokovic, tennis was dominated by the duopoly of Roger Federer and Rafael Nadal. Between them, they shared twenty out of twenty-three Grand Slams. That is an astonishing degree of predictability, even taking into account the superlative skill of Federer and Nadal.

What do we learn about tennis from that sequence of twenty Federer/Nadal titles out of a possible twenty-three? We know that tennis is far more determined by skill than it is by luck. The random element in tennis – umpiring mistakes, net cords, mishits that end up as winners – is rarely strong enough to dislodge the supremacy of the best players. Borg won Wimbledon five times in a row; so too did Federer. Four players – Jimmy Connors, Ivan Lendl, Pete Sampras and Roger Federer – have held the number-one world ranking for five years or more. Tennis is more chess than backgammon.

The good news is that tennis usually produces the 'right' or 'just' result because the better player nearly always wins. The bad news is that tennis can suffer from a lack of dramatic uncertainty. That's why tennis is prone to periods of dynastic dominance, in which the leading player is rarely dislodged. It also explains why many tennis matches – not the great ones, of course, which are as good as sport can get – are imbalanced and lack drama. One player is better, plays better, leads from the front, stays in front and inevitably wins the match. The rank underdog often loses so badly that he might as well not have bothered turning up. And we might as well not bother switching on.

There is insufficient luck built into the structure of the game, so a tennis mismatch can quickly descend into a highly probabilistic exercise in dominance. Even a dedicated tennis fan like me has to concede that it can be tennis's greatest flaw.

Does that matter? From a fan's perspective, yes, I think it does. Consider how the experience of watching Roger Federer has changed over the years. It's always been a pretty damn good experience, let's be clear about that. Federer fans can talk for hours about his balletic movement and joyous self-expression, miraculous points and impossible shots. The late novelist David Foster Wallace described them as 'Federer moments ... when the jaw drops and eyes protrude and sounds are made that bring spouses in from other rooms to see if you're OK'. Federer embodies the style and grace of the perfect amateur with the consistency and relentlessness of the ultimate professional.

But the real joy of watching Federer – for me, at least – has come later in his career, beginning in around 2008. What changed? Federer suddenly found himself under intense pressure, first from Rafael Nadal and then from Novak Djokovic. Tournaments ceased being mere Federer coronations; they became genuine contests. That shift made me view Federer differently, too. It took the uncertainty of real rivalry, not the inevitability of a long reign, to make his excellence truly interesting. I'd always admired Federer. But now I started to watch his matches with the dedication of a real fan. Paradoxically, it had taken the ascent of Nadal to make me fully appreciate Federer.

I don't think my experiences are untypical. The same logic explains why tennis relies to an unusual degree on the existence of great rivalries, not just Federer v Nadal, but also Borg v McEnroe and Sampras v Agassi. There isn't much of a luck factor in tennis, so optimal uncertainty relies on two perfectly matched players.

The problem, as you can imagine, is that it's pretty hard to arrange a perfectly poised rivalry all the time. We've been *lucky* that the careers of Federer and Nadal have coincided.

III

I am walking around a parade-ring full of racehorses with one of the greatest jump jockeys of all time. A. P. McCoy has been champion jockey for fifteen consecutive years, and he has the air of a champion. It's not so much what he says or does. It's more that McCoy has the kind of frank, openly tough face that suggests he is impervious to pain and discomfort. He has needed to be. As we walk around the trainer Jonjo O'Neill's magnificent stables in Gloucestershire, McCoy tells me how he has broken just about every bone in his body. But none of the setbacks held him down for long. He has now won over 3,000 races.

And yet for all his talent and toughness, one thing eluded McCoy: the Grand National. In his fourteen attempts at winning the National, he never did better than third. Speaking to him about his astonishing career, one thing became clear very quickly. For all his success, those fourteen years of failing to win the National had eaten away at him. He repeatedly called the National 'the greatest horse-race in the world'. It was hard for this serial winner to accept that he had struggled to win the biggest race of all.

Why did this champion jockey, with nothing left to prove, care so much about one race? And why do so many racing fans agree with him? What's so special about the National that makes it 'the people's race'? Is it the fact that the most fancied horse always wins? Far from it. Look at the odds of the last ten horses that won the National. Red Marauder

33–1; Bindaree 20–1; Monty's Pass 16–1; Amberleigh House 16–1; Hedgehunter 7–1; Numbersixvalverde 11–1; Silver Birch 33–1; Comply or Die 7–1; Mon Mome 100–1; Don't Push It 10–1.

It's difficult to think of an elite sporting event that is harder to predict. The National is a handicap, of course, so the best horses have to carry extra weight. But other factors operate as even more effective levellers. The huge field (forty horses) runs 4 miles and 856 yards with thirty brutally challenging fences. That causes about half the horses to fall every year. As a result, surprises inevitably come into play: if there are no favourites left standing, outsiders priced at 33–1 and 100–1 inevitably have a much greater chance of winning. As A. P. McCoy put it to me, 'You need luck to win the National. You need the horse in front of you not to fall.'

If you wanted to reduce the chances of Roger Federer and Rafael Nadal winning every tennis tournament, what could be more efficient than making them play on such an uneven court that half the players in the tournament (randomly selected) had to retire through injury? That would be a pretty effective leveller.

Perhaps the excessive unpredictability of the National is why racing experts regard the Cheltenham Gold Cup as arguably a greater horse-race. It is certainly more predictable. Between 2000 and 2010 all ten winners of the Gold Cup started in the first three in the betting. With a smaller field and more conventional fences, outstanding horses face a lower risk of being hobbled by bad luck. That's why the Gold Cup is probably a fairer judge of racing excellence.

But it is the National that captures the nation's attention. The 2011 Grand National was watched by 8.8 million people, a 65 per cent share of the TV audience at the time. The Gold Cup is loved by racing insiders. But its viewing figures hover only around 2 million.

Why is the National so deeply loved? Partly, it is because punters admire the sheer pluck needed to survive the biggest fences in the world. But there is a deeper factor: people thrill to the rogue influence of chance. Such a high degree of randomness is not good news if you're an expert wanting to make an accurate prediction. But it's tremendous if all you want is to lose yourself in the drama. We respond to the National's inherent uncertainty.

McCoy, by the way, won the National in 2010. Later that year, he was voted BBC Sports Personality of the Year, an award many people felt he had deserved to win long before.

IV

Although some seasons are inevitably exciting and closely fought, a recurrent criticism of Formula One is that it is prone to long, boring spells when one driver dominates too easily. Its critics go further, arguing that Formula One isn't a proper sport because the driver doesn't determine the outcome of the championship: the car is at least as significant.

Jenson Button, for example, was a largely unfulfilled talent until the manufacturer Brawn GP engineered a special feature for his car. In 2009, Button's car was fitted with an innovative diffuser design, which gave his car a major advantage over all the other teams. Button promptly won six of the first seven races. Eventually rival teams reconfigured their own diffusers to match Brawn's, and once the playing field had been levelled, Button's dominance ended: for the remaining ten races, he averaged only sixth position. But it was enough – all taken together – for him to win the Formula One title.

It is little wonder that critics argue Formula One is just an exercise in technical superiority. Yes, all the top drivers are highly skilled, and no one makes it on to the grid at Monte Carlo by chance alone. But it is the car, many insist, that usually makes the critical difference. Cynics say the importance of drivers is exaggerated by the racing industry to provide human-interest stories, to give the media something to talk about. After all, who wants to interview an engine?

This analysis of Formula One has found an unlikely new ally: the controller of Formula One, Bernie Ecclestone. He has suggested that Formula One races are becoming so predictable that something must be done. His answer is that it ought to rain more. 'Wet races are always the most exciting,' as he put it. Even Formula One, though, is unable to arrange a contract with the weather. So Ecclestone suggested that rain should be artificially supplied by a trackside sprinkler system.

What is so good about rain (both real and artificial)? It has three advantages. In dry weather, all the drivers tend to follow the same line on the corners of the race circuit. Effectively, every car plots the same path, without deviation or individuality – a bit like slot cars in old Scalextric kits. Wet weather makes it much harder to follow these established footprints.

Secondly, rain magnifies the uncertainty by increasing the likelihood of crashes. Thirdly, rain makes team tactics much harder to plan. As it is impossible to know exactly when it might begin to rain, the decision about when to change tyres becomes exposed to random forces. If you change to dry-weather tyres, and it rains, you are stuffed. If you change to wet-weather tyres, and it stays dry, you are lumbered with slow tread. In wet weather, instead of relying purely on technology, you are suddenly battling the gods.

The net effect of those three factors is that when it rains in Formula One, the best car is much more likely to be defeated. Rain levels the playing field. That is why Ecclestone advocates the fake rain being switched on at random. It is vital that teams don't get a chance to arrange a rain strategy in advance – that would merely result in the best car devising an optimal strategy that protects its advantage. After all, the whole point of the sprinkler theory is to introduce a random element into an all too predictable sport. It's like adding a joker into a poker game because the best player keeps winning.

Common sense suggests that spraying the track with water is too mad ever to happen. It would represent a huge risk to the drivers' safety. A race official, having decided to switch on the sprinklers and having thereby caused a fatal accident, might find himself charged with manslaughter.

But the mere existence of the sprinkler theory is an intriguing admission that Formula One is prone to failing in an unusual way. It can become weighted too far towards superiority, and too little towards luck. Ecclestone's comments were an endorsement of randomness in a sport that is usually wedded to technology.

Apple had to make the iPod seem less random to make it feel random. Formula One is considering making itself more random to make it feel like a sport.

V

In 2010, England failed lamentably in their attempt to win the football World Cup. Germany, once again, killed off English hopes with a devastating 4–1 victory on 27 June. But much of the controversy after the match focused on a disallowed goal. In the thirty-eighth minute, the England midfielder Frank Lampard struck a fierce long-range shot that appeared, to the naked eye, clearly to have crossed the goal-line. The referee saw things differently, and failed to award the goal.

Many English fans felt that this example of appalling luck had deprived England of a chance to get back into the game. The gods, once again, had conspired against us. (My personal view was that Lampard's shot deserved a goal, and certainly *was* a goal, but the wrong decision was highly unlikely to have changed the result because Germany were far better than England.) More importantly, millions of disappointed England fans had specific targets for their grievances. First, lady luck; second, bad refereeing; third, the refusal by Sepp Blatter, the head of world football, to introduce goal-line technology to reduce the chances of such errors. It was a seductive trio of arguments, particularly if you were an England fan.

But would reducing the role of luck in football really serve to make it a better spectacle overall? First, we should examine whether football is unusually susceptible to being influenced by the luck of decisive refereeing errors and other distorting interventions by chance.

Every sport, of course, has an element of chance. The question is how much. A lucky goal in Australian Rules Football (six points) is worth on average a fifteenth of a team's total score. A lucky basket (two points) in basketball is worth around a fortieth of the team's likely total score. A lucky point in tennis is worth about a hundredth of all the total number of points won by a victorious player.

Football, in contrast, is obviously at the opposite end of the spectrum. A football goal has the highest value of any sporting currency. Even a run in baseball, which is very precious, is not quite as valuable as a football goal. Just one of these precious things is often enough to determine a whole match.

The huge size of football's currency unit – the goal – makes luck a far greater force in football than in other sports. A net cord, we already know, can randomly determine a single tennis point. But it would be staggeringly unlikely that one player could get enough lucky net cords in one match to change the result. In football, by contrast, one lucky score is all you need. That is why refereeing decisions in football become so controversial. Listen to Arsène Wenger, listen to Sir Alex Ferguson. A wrong offside decision or a penalty is far more likely to influence the final result of a football match than a misjudged 'out' call in tennis. A wrong call in tennis determines one point out of hundreds; a wrong penalty in football may well be the only score of the day. Football's clunky system of counting builds chance into the structure of the whole sport.

It's a good rule of thumb: the higher the number in a sport's scoreline, the larger the probability that the score was determined by ability rather than luck. In high-scoring sports, the chance is 'averaged out', in the language of statistics. That's why sports like tennis are so predictable. But in football, because goals are so enormously rare, the result of the match is more open to chance than it is in almost any other sport.

The Notts County manager Jimmy Sirrel expressed an admirable sentiment when he claimed that 'The best team always wins and the rest is just gossip.' But the facts are against him. The better team often loses. That one team can be outplayed for eighty-eight minutes, scrabble a lucky goal and still win one–nil is an ever-present footballing narrative. Underdog teams, underdog fans, underdog coaches: where other sports send them into despair, football leaves them in with a chance.

You might think that this openness to chance would count against football, that we would tire of its injustices. We don't. They enthral us. Football, of course, is the world's favourite game. Trying to explain that popularity would take a whole book, but we can sketch a few explanations in broad outline: it's cheap, it's easy to explain, it's straightforward to play at a low level, it doesn't require sophisticated technology, the pitch is a simple rectangle and the goals can be constructed from nothing more high-tech than four old jumpers placed on the ground.

But I think we have missed an equally significant explanation for football's massive popularity: its structural capacity to produce upsets, surprises and underdog victories. Usually, this structural uncertainty is expressed in whimsical terms of regret, as though it is frustrating that football should be so intractable, so slippery, so hard to master and control. The brilliant football writer Simon Kuper captured the sentiment of all pundits who've been asked to make predictions about an international football tournament:

The World Cup is a random event where after six or seven games anyone could win. Arsène Wenger points out that in a league any team can be leading the table after one month, because it's such a short sample period. Argentina has won two World Cups, Holland none, but it easily could have been the other way around. It's really a fool's business to try to call it.

But consider the flipside of Kuper's argument. It is precisely because it is a fool's business to try to *call* the World Cup that it is such a sensible business to try to *watch* it, as one billion people did on the night of the final alone. Uncertainty is a pain to predict, but a joy to follow. Football is not the world's favourite game because it ensures that the best team always wins. It is the most popular sport because it accidentally ensures that the best team *doesn't* always win.

Correspondingly, its injustices are all part of football's magic. It's taken me too long to realize that. Interviewed on the *Today* programme during the early stages of the 2010 World Cup, I was asked what changes I would make to improve the game as a spectacle. I replied, rashly, that I'd place the goal posts further apart so that there are more goals. (In my defence, it was ludicrously early in the morning.)

I was, of course, completely wrong. Football relies upon the fact that the paucity of goals provides an endless supply of upsets. The fewer the goals the greater the uncertainty, and the greater the uncertainty, the more justified hope there is for underdogs and outsiders. Football is the most popular game in the world for a very good reason: by extending realistic hope to lesser teams, it is the most democratic.

We want a happy equilibrium. For a sport to have optimal uncertainty, the better team should win most times, but it shouldn't win every time. We want to watch a game that seems to be 'just' most of the time. But not so fair that it is too predictable. We seek a winning compromise between probabilistic determinism (boring) and pure randomness (equally boring). After all, we won't pay satellite subscriptions to watch the favourite win every time. But nor will we pay money to watch a random spin of the roulette board.

The appeal of football, its fans may be surprised to learn, was best expressed by Winston Churchill, even though he was talking about life rather than sport. 'Without a measureless and perpetual uncertainty, the drama of human life would be destroyed.'

VI

You have, I'm sure, spotted the flaw in my argument: the Premier League.

Here is the list of teams that won the Premier League in the sixteen years before the 2011–12 season: Manchester United, Manchester United, Arsenal, Manchester United, Manchester United, Manchester United, Arsenal, Manchester United, Arsenal, Chelsea, Chelsea, Manchester United, Manchester United, Manchester United, Chelsea, Manchester United. Not very unpredictable, is it? As I write, it is seventeen years since any team won English football's top prize that wasn't called Chelsea, Manchester United or Arsenal. It is nine years since anyone broke up the duo of Manchester

United and Chelsea. Few sports leagues in the world have less uncertainty than the Premier League when it comes to the destiny of the title.

And it's hard to avoid the conclusion, I'm afraid, that this predictability is reinforced by financial inequality. The economist Stefan Szymanski studied the correlation between wages and league position in the Premier League. He found that spending accounted for 89 per cent of the variation in league position. Unsurprisingly, the top four wage bills are currently those of Chelsea, Manchester United, Arsenal and Manchester City. There is a huge correlation between a football club's cash and its success.

So how can I explain the fact that the Premier League's predictability has not (yet) affected its huge global popularity? I can't. And it remains my view that the Premier League would be even more successful if it had more competitive equipoise. If more teams had a chance of winning the title, it would be an even more formidable sporting product.

But even if the title is limited to an extremely exclusive club of three teams, individual matches in the Premier League continue to benefit from football's innate uncertainty. Let's take a random weekend of Premier League results. Let's go for the first week of March 2011. How many of the matches went against form and were won by the lower-placed team? Fourth-placed Chelsea beat first-placed Manchester United. Tenth-placed Stoke couldn't beat seventeenth-placed West Brom. Third-placed Man City couldn't beat thirteenth-placed Fulham. Nineteenth-placed West Ham beat sixth-placed

Liverpool. Twelfth-placed Aston Villa beat fourteenth-placed Blackburn. Eleventh-placed Sunderland beat eighth-placed Everton. Ninth-placed Newcastle drew with seventh-placed Bolton. Last-placed Wigan were defeated by the leaders Manchester United. Eighteenth-placed Wolves beat fifteenth-placed Blackpool.

So six matches ended in a result rather than a draw. Four of those six were won by the lower-placed team, only two by the 'superior' side. You could say the underdogs beat the favourites 4–2. If you turned up to those six matches wanting to experience the dramatic uncertainty of not knowing who would win, there is a good chance you got your money's worth.

It's true, over the course of a whole season, that teams settle into positions that are 89 per cent correlated to their financial muscle. But over the short run – *on any given Saturday* – even the Premier League, for all its financial disequilibrium, can't trump football's ability to produce surprises. So as long as fans retain short memories and the capacity for hope over experience, the Premier League will continue to benefit from the luck factor.

Football doesn't require fewer errors and more justice. It just needs to stay sufficiently open to luck so that no one gets too bored.

14

When there really is no such thing as luck

I

Where does it lead us, people complain, all this believing in luck? What's the take-home message, the practical benefit, what are we supposed to *do* about it? In one sense, the question is not relevant here. This is not a self-help book that promises to unlock the secret of how to win, or how to get rich, still less how to become a genius.

Thinking about luck does, however, teach us something about how success happens. The best example comes from the natural world: consider how advances in understanding evolution have changed the way we think about success in that sphere. Before Darwin, it was assumed that successful organisms must have been created by design, by the hand of a single creator. The nineteenth-century theologian the Rev. William Paley used the metaphor of a man who stumbles on a watch lying on a heath. The intricacy of the watch provided indisputable evidence of design. By the same logic, according to Paley and many who thought the same way, the complexity of the natural world was evidence of a Designer, and hence provided proof of the existence of a Divine Being.

Darwin and his followers would throw Paley's argument back in his face. Evolution was shown to be caused by the *interaction* of chance and selection. And the result of that interaction produces better-organized, superior results than anyone's conscious process could allow. For example, all the resources of modern optics and information technology cannot yet rival the sensitivity and flexibility of the eye. Evolution is smarter than any single mind could be. 'The blind watchmaker', in Richard Dawkins's memorable phrase, is more skilled than any sighted manufacturer.

The point here is that we cannot say the successful evolution of an organism is caused by 60 per cent chance mutation and 40 per cent selection. Chance and selection do not mix in evolution. They interact to produce something quite new. Success, to use a metaphor from chemistry rather than biology, is not a mixture. It is a compound. Luck is a crucial ingredient that goes into making an end-product that may be unrecognizable from its constituent parts.

Something similar happens with success in other spheres. The economist John Kay has used evolutionary arguments to explain how great businesses become successful. He criticizes the view that success in business must be derived from a single, shaping vision or mission statement that is then relentlessly 'executed': 'We tend to infer design where there was only adaptation and improvisation, and to attribute successful business outcomes to the realisation of some deliberate plan. Such thinking repeats Paley's error. Large and complex corporations not only are, but could only be, the product of incremental change and adaptation.'

Many of those adaptations – modifications that improve the fit between the company and the environment in which it operates – will be accidental rather than deliberate. In business, as Kay puts it, 'There is a better shortened explanation of the success of evolution than the survival of the fittest. It is that "evolution is smarter than you".' Successful businesses, Kay implies, should focus more on being open to innovation and adaption – both deliberate and accidental – and less on the ghastly fad for mission statements and 'blue-sky thinking'.

I would make the same argument about a successful individual life. We are too easily misled by the biographies of great men and women who claim, after the fact, to have meticulously planned their ascent, to have converged on success like soldiers finding a flag in an army-training exercise. The origins of success are usually much more subtle and more complex. Successful people, by being open to opportunity and exposing themselves to chance, take new directions that prove more fruitful than anyone could have predicted. A life does not follow a course. We change in many ways as we grow. A missed opportunity represents the failure to evolve into a different, better person.

Successful lives are adaptable, in every sense.

But many people still think that it is backward and passive to believe in luck, that the idea doesn't quite belong in the modern world. We tend to associate admissions of powerlessness such as luck and fate with outdated and long-abandoned systems of thought.

The Greeks, of course, were obsessed with the concepts of luck and fate. They developed a series of overlapping words, and indeed deities, to describe various forms of luck. The supernatural element in a man's experience was determined by his *daimon*. Whatever happens without you intending it to happen was described as *tyche*, roughly analogous to chance or luck. Your *moira* was your allotted portion or share. But the concept could also be personified in the form of the Moirai, or the Fates. In Homer, Zeus himself seems to be subject to Fate most of the time, but some passages equate it with his will. Fate was sometimes a divinity, sometimes an independent force − arbitrary, deaf to prayer and even more powerful than the gods.

Who wants to return to such a superstitious, pessimistic, fate-ridden view of life? What could be less fitted for our society? After all, 'Modernity is the transition from fate to choice,' as Jonathan Sacks put it. That is even the view of some scholars of the classical world, who berate the ancients for their preoccupation with luck. In *The Greeks and the Irrational*, the Oxford Professor E. R. Dodds argued that the Greeks came very close to creating a rational world in which free will, not fate, dominated their intellectual mindset. Dodds admired the less well-known strand within classical thought that was contemptuous of people who blamed their luck. Democritus argued that the idea of luck is merely a human invention to provide people with an excuse for their own failings. Another proverb urged self-responsibility rather than belief in luck: 'Never blame me, Tyche [Fortune], for I have no strength.'

Sadly, according to Dodds, the classical world then lost its way when it embraced luck and fate, a symptom of feeble irrationality. The Greeks had come close to embracing the noble idea of free will, before reverting to superstition and astrology: 'The individual had been face to face with his own intellectual freedom, and now he turned and bolted from the horrid prospect – better the rigid determinism of the Astrological Fate than the terrifying burden of daily responsibility.' According to Dodds, the Greek obsession with luck and divination was a great missed opportunity in the history of human thought. Astrology 'fell upon the Hellenistic mind as a new disease falls upon some remote island people'. In this version of history, luck was an illness that knocked the West off course, the intellectual equivalent of the influenza epidemic that would later ravage the Americas.

But not every classical scholar has been so quick to criticize the intellectual and moral consequences of believing in luck. The philosopher Martha Nussbaum, for example, rejects the Platonic idea that the conditions required for a good life (*eudaimonia*) are entirely within our control. In *The Fragility of Goodness*, Nussbaum endorses the Aristotelian idea that circumstances matter. Rationality and virtue alone are not enough; you also need luck:

> That I am an agent, but also a plant; that much that I did not make goes into making me whatever I shall be praised or blamed for being; that an event that simply happens to me may, without my consent, alter my life; that it is equally problematic to entrust one's good to friends, lovers, or country and to try to have a good life without them – all these I take to be not just the material of tragedy, but everyday facts of lived practical reason.

In Nussbaum's account, it is the control freak in human nature – not Dodds's 'irrational' idea of luck – that causes ethical problems. The idea that good living requires good luck is a civilizing concept. Nussbaum seeks to revive the idea that 'human worth is inseparable from vulnerability . . . a rationality whose nature is not to attempt to seize, hold, trap and control'. Understanding the role of luck, by forcing us to acknowledge our vulnerability, should make us more human.

Perhaps the only fair way to settle the argument – between Dodds, who interprets luck as a dangerous irrationality, and Nussbaum who believes it is a civilizing force for good – is to examine how other societies that *lacked* the concept of luck got along.

III

In 1926, the young English anthropologist E. E. Evans-Pritchard went to live with the Azande tribe in the Sudan. The fieldwork would become the basis of his doctorate and of his influential book *Witchcraft, Oracles and Magic among the Azande*. Evans-Pritchard made some intriguing observations, in particular about the causes and consequences of believing in witchcraft:

> For a Zande almost every happening which is harmful to him is due to the evil disposition of someone else . . . In our own society only certain misfortunes are believed to be due to the wickedness of other people . . . But in Zandeland all misfortunes are due to witchcraft . . . Witch finding, as a practice of allocating responsibility, turns what might otherwise be an accident or random misfortune into an action.

What we would call luck or misfortune was not interpreted as luck or misfortune among the Azande. Indeed, they had no word for luck or chance. Luck was absent from their vocabulary because it was not relevant to their view of the world. Instead of luck, they had witches. When a Zande went to visit a witch, he attempted to identify who was bewitching him. He was seeking someone to hold to account, someone to blame. In the absence of the concept of luck, everything that went wrong must have originated in specific and deliberate ill-will by another Zande.

Evans–Pritchard found that witchcraft provided causal links for anything that needed to be explained. It was 'the ideological pivot around which swings the lengthy social procedure from death to vengeance'. The Azande found blame, created culprits, demanded redress – in general, created responsibility – for events that Evans–Pritchard didn't think warranted any moral blame.

What were the social consequences of believing that every event must be deliberately caused by someone else? What is it like to live without a concept of luck? Evans–Pritchard found that Azande life was characterized by mistrust, suspicion and jealousy between neighbours. No one ever simply died in Zandeland; death was never just an accident. Someone was always to blame.

The Cambridge academic James Laidlaw used Evans–Pritchard's Azande study to explore whether Western society, too, is producing an unhelpful surfeit of what he called 'agency'. Are we, too, moving towards believing that everything is caused by deliberate human intervention? What happens when there is too much agency, and not enough luck?

Laidlaw goes on to argue that our own society is undergoing its own kind of 'proliferation of agency'. Television adverts ask you to consider taking legal action to gain 'compensation' for injuries that you'd not previously considered to have been anyone's fault. If you can find a causal link, however tenuous, between an ailment and your employer, you could benefit financially. In effect, the law firm is asking you to turn an accident into an act of 'agency' for which someone is directly responsible.

If Andrew, my American friend, had not been lucky enough to receive superb CPR, if he had suffered terrible brain damage, his wife doubtless would have been bombarded with legal approaches pushing them to sue the paramedics. There is some truth, too, in the caricature of 'the media witch-hunt'. Not everything that goes wrong must have a culprit. But the search for a face on to which we can pin all our fury appeals to the vengeful side of human nature. We like to have a villain in the stocks – even if, in our heart of hearts, we suspect that the causal link between the crime and the culprit is unconvincing.

IV

There are other tribal cultures that do not possess the concept of luck. For the Dobuan people of Papua New Guinea, there is simply no such word. In the absence of luck, it is impossible that anyone can ever be struck by lightning without an enemy having willed it out of envy. A neighbour's harvest can only be better than yours due to black magic.

In his book *Envy*, the sociologist Helmut Schoeck argued that societies lacking the idea of luck find it hard to develop enterprise and aspiration. Why? Without any means of explaining the differing lots that fall to people, society remains dominated by envy. Fear of being envied makes people fearful of doing well. Averageness becomes the stifling ideal. Conversely, Schoeck argued that luck civilizes. He saw the classical concept of Fortune as driving the evolution of the Western world:

> Every culture must have an explanation to offer to its members for the varying lots that fall to them. Some cultures have been successful in this task, others relatively unsuccessful. The path of inequality is less rugged for the man living in a community whose culture has evolved conceptions, such as varying degrees of luck, which can assuage his own conscience and disarm the envious.

The German classicist M. P. Nilsson went further. He traced the Western idea of justice to the concept of Fortune. Homer used the term hubris to mean presumption or trespass. The classical concept of fate – *moira* – was always expressed in phrases that meant 'part, share or portion'. A man who took more than his due risked tempting fate.

We are used to thinking that the more free will we have the better, that it is always better for humans to think they have control over events. We tend to consider the growth of 'agency' – the opposite of blind luck – to be synonymous with the progress of human civilization. But the lessons of sociology and anthropology suggest we shouldn't interpret words like luck, fortune and chance as signs of backwardness. In fact, we should be more worried when we *stop* believing in the idea of luck. At a time when millions of people indulge in the meretricious book *The Secret*, that moment may be approaching fast.

V

When my broken ankle failed to heal in time for me to play any part in the rest of the 2008 season, some people suggested I should take legal action against the medical staff who'd treated me. But what would happen if I had brought and won such a case? There would be an attempt to identify one single guilty individual instead of a hazy sense of shared responsibility. There would be a quest for a villain rather than an acknowledgement of misfortune. In the legal version of events, following a hunt for causes, my case would have to convert bad luck into individual responsibility. I didn't want to do that because I held a different view. Lots of people misjudged my ankle injury, including me. No one willed it to happen. It was an accident.

And, as I found out while living under the utopian ideals of Kent's Core Covenant in 1999, it's not just that you and I need luck individually. We need luck in a much broader sense, too.

Since writing those words, I have witnessed first-hand how one family's interpretation of luck and justice led them to act with extraordinary grace and generosity of spirit.

It's not often you get on so well with strangers at a wedding party that they invite you to stay at their house. But that is exactly what happened when I was a guest at a wedding on a high summer's day in Sussex. I sat next to Joan and Roderick Noble. We talked about cricket, travel and families. Joan spoke lovingly and proudly of her son, Ian, a brilliant medic about the same age as me. I remember her saying that we would get on, that Ian was a keen cricket fan who loved going to Lord's. I left the wedding early to catch a plane, but only after I'd arranged to meet up with the Nobles soon after the wedding.

A few weeks later, I heard that their son Ian had been killed. He had been hit by a car while riding across London on his scooter. Everton Wright, a thirty-two-year-old plumber from Croydon, had turned across the carriageway without seeing Ian on his scooter in the bus lane. Ian was thrown eight feet into the air and suffered fatal head injuries.

'When you lose a child, you think about it all the time, it just never leaves you,' Joan says. But when the driver was convicted of careless driving, the Nobles made an extraordinary intervention. They wrote to the judge. They told him: 'Our lives are wrecked. It is unlikely we will ever get over this loss.' Yet they asked the judge not to send the driver to prison. They felt strongly that their son would not have wanted Wright to go to jail; instead Ian would have wanted him 'to do something for the good of society'. Their wish was granted. The judge thanked the Nobles for their 'quiet dignity', observed that Wright had shown deep remorse and pleaded guilty – and sentenced him to 150 hours of community work.

'I can't see the benefit in sending someone to prison for an accident,' Joan explains. 'He made a hell of a mistake. How many of us have been in that position? He's got to live with that for the rest of his life. Nothing is going to bring Ian back. We didn't want retribution for retribution's sake. One of the first things I asked the policeman when he came to tell us was, "What did the driver say? Was he upset?" The policeman replied that the driver had been terribly concerned. In fact, he wanted to go to the hospital with Ian. He wasn't a bad guy.'

Joan shrugs off the idea that they did something heroic. 'I was stunned by the media attention. It seemed the most natural thing in the world. Sending someone to jail would just have caused even more misery.' How could a family forgive the man who killed their precious son? 'It's not about forgiveness, because it was an accident,' Ian's younger brother Jamie said after the trial.

The Nobles founded a bursary fund in their son's name. It has raised over £100,000 to assist poorer medical students to further their studies at Sheffield University. King's College Hospital in London has also set up an award. The Ian Noble award will be given to the foundation-year doctor who has done the most for the hospital. Joan is clearly deeply proud. 'It's quite staggering, really.'

What a depth of humanity and civility was revealed in the responses of the Noble family. The ability to distinguish between differing kinds of guilt; the capacity to form moral judgements despite bitter and irreparable anguish; the determination to make practical advances despite terrible loss; the ability to accept as well as to act; an awareness of chance, not just of agency.

We all want to believe in the ascent of man, that people are becoming kinder and more humane, that civilization is advancing. But even the firmest belief can be shaken. It isn't easy to retain faith. The actions of the Nobles have reaffirmed mine.

15

What-ifs

1

No regrets, no looking back, no what-ifs. That's what people say. No wallowing in the past, no harking back to forks in the road, no imaginary trips along roads untravelled. The implication is that reflecting on what might have been is necessarily melancholic, even self-pitying.

But what if the what-if, so to speak, prompts you to feel grateful rather than embittered? Why should counterfactuals, as historians call what-ifs, lead us to regrets rather than towards gratitude? Consider the what-ifs implicit in this book. What if I'd been educated at a school that wasn't so good at producing professional cricketers? I might well not have played first-class cricket, let alone for England.

Playing for England at the Oval in 2003, I was wrongly given out LBW. With today's rules, I would be able to review the decision and would be recalled. Not then. I trudged back to the pavilion and never played for England again. What if? Yes, I might have played more for England. But if I had toured the world with the England team, then I almost certainly wouldn't have been in the right place at the right time to meet – well, we'll come to that in a moment.

What if I hadn't broken my ankle in 2008? Had I not broken my ankle, I would have had more good days on the cricket field, perhaps better days than any of those that had come before. Middlesex went on to win the Twenty20 competition. The final – yes, at the Rose Bowl – was a wonderful game that went down to the last ball, and I'd be lying if I pretended I wouldn't have loved to be out on the pitch. It was Middlesex's first trophy for fifteen years.

But what if I hadn't broken my ankle? I might have found it hard to leave cricket at all. I could easily have stayed too long for my own good. Why? Because I can see now what I daren't admit to myself when I was still playing. I can see that my relationship with cricket was not really a professional calculation at all. I never weighed up the pros and cons of staying in professional sport, or whether I would have a more fulfilling life elsewhere, or even make more money. I never admitted it to anyone at the time, but cricket always seemed to me an alternative to normal life rather than a part of it. I never imagined, for example, that I could have got married when I was still playing. When I was a cricketer, I felt I was too self-obsessed to be a husband.

Cricket, now I think about it, wasn't a job at all. It was a love affair. It was a lifelong obsession of mine that I never viewed rationally. Over the years, with failures and disappointments, cricket gradually loosened its grip. But it never entirely let go of me. Had it not been for the snap and the pain at Lord's on 12 June 2008 I might never have managed to end the affair. Thirteen years is a long time to have a job that revolves around hitting a piece of leather. It is a long time for a life to be framed and defined by the rhythms of practice sessions, or to be punctuated by the loneliness of checking into soulless hotels and filling up the car with petrol late at night at motorway service stations after last-ball defeats.

But when you are in love with a game, as I was, you spend vast amounts of time and energy thinking about where you can go together. You and cricket, arm in arm, all disagreements settled, all betrayals forgotten. There is always next year, always tomorrow, always the next innings. That image, of total success and perfect happiness, with applause in your ears and your bat raised aloft, is the snapshot that you keep in your mind's eye. It is what prevents you from starting afresh, somewhere new.

Friends of mine sometimes reminded me that I used to say I'd give up cricket as soon as I wasn't in contention for the England team. But I found that there was always a reason to think that that moment had never quite arrived. I was hitting the ball better, I had made a new technical improvement, I was thinking more clearly. This would be my year, that was always my mindset. In truth, it wasn't only the prospect of playing for England that kept me going. It was the game itself.

What happens when an affair has run its course, when it is

no longer good for you, but you can't bring yourself to do anything about it? Without a broken bone to make the decision for me, my relationship with cricket would have been hard to break off. The pleasure of timing a cricket ball, of feeling the tap of the bat on hard soil on a summer's day, the thrill of being in control of an innings and a match, the smell of cut grass in spring – all these things might have retained their grip on my inner-adolescent for too long.

Sometimes something bad must happen before something good can happen. Breaking my ankle was that lucky break. And if I hadn't broken my ankle, I wouldn't have thought about luck in the way that I now do. I wouldn't have realized that conscious decisions and choices – in which I'd always placed such deep faith – are infinitely vulnerable to circumstances beyond our control. I wouldn't have grown up. And I wouldn't have written this book.

11

When a team-mate was picked for England, I arranged a celebratory drink at my west London flat. But my colleague didn't have time to drive back to his home in Clapham before coming to mine. So he arrived explaining that he wouldn't be able to drink alcohol as he would have to drive home later.

Knowing how much it means to get picked for England, and strongly suspecting he'd want to mark the occasion with a glass of something, I suggested that he should leave his car on a parking meter outside my house and then get a cab home after dinner. We could celebrate that night, and I would drive his car back to Clapham for him the following morning.

The first half of the plan worked well, as it was always likely to do. The second half quickly turned unpleasant – my being woken up the following morning by an early alarm call, then climbing into a friend's car armed only with an A–Z map and a strong coffee. It was the hottest day of the summer, and I was quickly lost in unfamiliar streets on the other side of town. I eventually found his house and returned his car keys. Now I had to get from Clapham to Kent, where my family were gathered at my parents' house for lunch. Congratulating myself on my good deed in returning the car, I rewarded myself by deciding to get a taxi to Waterloo station. One thing I was definitely not going to endure on a sweltering Saturday morning: the Northern Line.

Half an hour passed waiting for a cab. No luck. No cab. Cursing my luck, I retreated to Clapham tube station. The Northern Line was, of course, suffering major delays. I was in tube hell. One change of line was followed by another, each greeted by descending then ascending escalators and the familiar blasts of hot condensed filthy air.

Emerging into daylight again, I sprinted from Waterloo tube to Waterloo East train station to catch the midday train. I eventually collapsed, dishevelled and shambolic, into an empty carriage on the Connex South Eastern commuter train from London to Hastings.

The carriage was almost empty. There was one other person, sitting in the same cluster of seats, diagonally opposite me, looking out of the window. She was in her early twenties, with blue eyes and wavy Giselle-like brown hair, the embodiment of elegance and poise. Briefly peering over the top of her book, she seemed as serene as I was bedraggled. Even Cary Grant, escaping New York by train in Hitchcock's *North by Northwest*, wasn't this lucky when he found himself sitting opposite Eva Marie Saint.

I am not, I promise, the kind of man who makes a habit of speaking to strangers on trains. But this was different. How, then, to break the ice? The ticket inspector quickly arrived. 'I don't need to see your tickets, I just need to know where you're going,' he rather weakly suggested. I found myself in the unusual position of wanting to give a ticket inspector a hug of thanks for inviting such an easy riposte. 'Is this a new era of trust on national rail?' I said aloud in my best ticket-inspector voice after he had gone. 'If you know where you were going, surely that's proof enough that you've bought a ticket?'

It was enough, just enough, to prompt a kind of laugh from the beautiful stranger. Depending on which witness you speak to – there were only two, me and her – it was either an amused smirk or else an uncontrolled outburst of genuine laughter. No matter. We spent the rest of journey chatting and laughing. Forty minutes later we alighted at the same platform. Three years later we were married.

The chances of me being on that train were almost zero. So I owe several thank-yous to unknowing matchmakers who pushed me in the direction of the Connex South Eastern commuter train: that week's opposition for losing the match a day early, giving me a free day to visit my family in Kent; my team-mate for his good form; the England selectors for picking him (well, they did owe me one); London's cab drivers for neglecting south London that day; the tube operators for organizing such helpful delays; the ticket collector for his eccentricity.

Rebecca's journey had been as unlikely as mine. Returning from France on her way to Durham, she had changed plans at the last minute, entirely on a whim, to visit her family in Kent. Two highly unlikely journeys had to happen at exactly the same time. And they did.

Friends have asked if I think it was fate that I was on the train that day. Given such long odds, we naturally fall back on phrases like 'always meant to be' or 'romantic destiny'. I'm not so sure. The idea of destiny suggests that it was inevitable I would have met and married Rebecca, that the story could only have ended that way. Destiny, it seems to me, is only a short jump from a sense of entitlement.

I see it differently. There was no guiding hand of fate. It was much more interesting than that. It was luck.

Acknowledgements

I am very grateful to:

Dr John Adamson, Simon Barnes, Professor Andrew Berry, Michael Binyon, Dr Woody Brock, Nigel Clarke, Dr Tony Collins, Cutler Cook, David and Tink Davis, Matt Drew, Professor William James Earle, Andrew Gaines, Ed Gorman, Gideon Haigh, Professor Richard Holt, Dr James Laidlaw, Dominic Lawson, Mark Lawson, Bronwen Maddox, Professor Ian Martin, Adrian Michaels, Colin Montgomorie, Matthew Parris, Neil Pearson, Farris Salah, Dr Anthony Seldon, Vikram Seth, Professor Brendan Simms, Mark Skipworth, Dr Adrian Smith, Professor Stefan Szymanski, Professor Nassim Nicholas Taleb, Professor Robert Travers, Erica Wagner, Professor James Watson, Richard Woolhouse.

Steve Darlow kindly introduced me to Bill Green, whose memory and energy were inspiring.

Matt Denhart provided invaluable help in compiling and collating the statistics about past and present England internationals.

This book grew partly out of a series of conversations over many years with Dr Woody Brock. He introduced me to Professor Kenneth J. Arrow and Professor Mordecai Kurz, who were both very generous with their time when I visited them at Stanford University. It would take another book to do justice to those conversations.

I was very fortunate to be given such a warm welcome to *The Times* by James Harding, Keith Blackmore, Roger Alton and Emma Tucker. I also learnt a great deal from *The Times* leader writers: Daniel Finkelstein, Philip Collins, Camilla Cavendish, Joe Joseph, Oliver Kamm, Hugo Rifkind and Philip Howard, who kindly put me in touch with Peter Jones. Matthew Syed generously shared his research about British Olympians.

Several people read parts or all of the manuscript, making extremely helpful corrections and recommendations: Professor John Kay, Martin Trew, Matt Ridley, Dr John Taylor, Jonathan Smith, Becky Quintavalle, John Blundell and Rebecca Smith.

I am deeply indebted to my agent David Godwin, who was a brilliant, generous and wise presence throughout. It was partly a chance conversation with my colleague Ben Macintyre that led me to be published by Bloomsbury. Michael Fishwick instantly understood and expertly steered the book. Working with Nigel Newton, Richard Charkin, Anna Simpson, Henry Jeffreys, Tess Viljoen and Anya Rosenberg couldn't have been more fun. Real luck.

A NOTE ON THE AUTHOR

Ed Smith is an author and journalist, and a former international cricketer who represented England, Cambridge University, Kent and Middlesex, where he was captain for two seasons. Ed Smith's previous books include *Playing Hard Ball*, *On and Off the Field* – the Wisden Book of the Year and shortlisted for the William Hill Sports Book of the Year – and the critically acclaimed *What Sport Tells Us About Life*. After retiring from cricket Ed Smith became a leader writer for *The Times*. He is now a *Times* features writer, *GQ* columnist and writes for the *Spectator*. He appears regularly on the *Today* Programme and in 2010 he wrote and presented his first TV documentary for BBC1. Ed Smith lives in London.

A NOTE ON THE TYPE

The text of this book is set in Bembo. This type was first used in 1495 by the Venetian printer Aldus Manutius for Cardinal Bembo's *De Aetna*, and was cut for Manutius by Francesco Griffo. It was one of the types used by Claude Garamond (1480–1561) as a model for his Romain de l'Université, and so it was the forerunner of what became standard European type for the following two centuries. Its modern form follows the original types and was designed for Monotype in 1929.